CONTENTS

6 Introduction

14 How To...
15 Knit
24 Felt
25 Appliqué
26 Sew
28 Crochet

30 Made To Measure
Clothing for the
Discerning Craftster
32 Get Felt Up Mittens
34 Sew Pretty Pinny
36 Wings of Desire
38 The 'Tie It Up' Top
40 Unicorn Believer
42 Ra Ra Apron
43 Skinny Ribbing Scarf
44 Bow Down Belt
46 Eco Shopper

48 All That Glitters
Jewellery To Complement
The Look
50 Happy Hemper
52 Button Up Badge Necklace
53 Brazen Barbie Bling
54 Papier Mâché Jewellery
56 Knitted Floral Fancy
58 Ballsy Necklace
59 Blow Your Own
Trumpet Tiara
60 Beady Eyed Lizard
61 Vinyl Cuff
62 Papercut Necklace

64 Hipper Homes
Live Your Craft
66 Tasty T-Shirt Bath Mat
68 Decoupage Bowl
69 Hottie Cover
70 Barking Mad
Draught Excluder
72 Stick 'Em Up Buttons
74 Lullablind
76 Starlight Lantern
78 Origami Fairy Light Shades
80 From Rags to Riches
82 Car Boot Cake Stand
83 Chai Bath Teabags
84 Supermarket Soap
88 Lovely Lavender Sachets

89 Sticks & Stones
& Ice Cream Cones
The Random Bits
That Fill the Gaps
92 Fabulous Fleecy
Felted Flowers
94 Jumper Monkey
96 Record Breaking Notebooks
99 The Gin Binger's Booze Cosy
100 Aye Aye Sailor i-Pod Cosy
102 Recycled Tie Purses
104 Antenna Tag
106 Puppet Junkie
108 Nara Paintchip
Passport Holder
110 Hipster PDA

112 Small Wonders
Things to Make for
and with Kids
114 Horsing Around Sock Puppet
116 Hedgehog Puppet
118 Hanging in the Balance
120 Curtain Spiders
121 Jackito-Lanterns
122 Steiner Dolls
125 Beeswax Candles
126 Abbey Baby Bib
128 Pixie Bonnet
130 Frock Rocking in Smocking
133 Shadow Puppet Show
134 Eco Warrior Kite

136 Craft Web-Directory

140 Acknowledgements

MAKING STUFF

An Alternative
Craft Book

black dog
publishing

INTRODUCTION

Victoria Woodcock

Something strange happens whenever I mention the word 'craft'. People begin to smile, even snigger. Apparently they associate the word with church fetes, quilting bees, a baby's first birthday cross-stitch sampler, flower arranging.... Craft aficionado and contributor to this book, Camilla Stacey, sums up the misguided perception of craft: "Crafts are something that grandmas do, that the Women's Institute does—like mice made out of teasels!"

I am quite unpleasantly surprised. Haven't they seen the plethora of articles declaring knitting the new yoga? Over the past years national and local newspapers across the entire globe have commented on the trend. Goddamit, there have even been craft workshops in Topshop! Even some of those I have tried to influence don't quite get it: my friend Katy gave up knitting half way through her first scarf because "it's just not rock 'n' roll".

Au contraire dear Katy, welcome to the craft revolution! Allow me to break it down for you…

She's Crafty: The Story of Contemporary Craft

Back in the 1980s craft picked up a major contemporary cool credential—or sort of! In New York, a certain rapping, skate boarding, graffiti lovin' threesome released their album, *Licensed to Ill*, which featured a little ditty called "She's Crafty". In the Beastie Boys' lyrical masterpiece, crafty girl Lucy, ("but they called her loose") tempts B Boy MCA back to his place, but the next morning: "I found myself naked in the middle of the floor/ She had taken the bed and the chest of drawers/ The mirror, the TV, the guitar cord/ My remote control and my old skateboard."

Whilst the line "The girl is crafty as ice is cool" may read as a modern day craft mantra, I'm pretty sure the Beastie Boys didn't intend it thus. However, lady Lucy highlights the meaning of the word 'craft': it may mean skill and ability, but also guile and cunning. By flicking through the projects in this book it is easy to see that they are conceived using equal parts of guile and skill: old bed sheets become a shopping bag, ties take on a new lease of life as a coin purse, and worn out jumpers are turned into mittens, hot water bottle covers and even a cuddly monkey.

This duality is at the heart of contemporary craft and inspiring examples of dual-edged craftiness can be found long before the B Boys ever existed. During the World Wars, women became masterminds of 'make do and mend', so resourceful they fashioned up sexy knickers out of parachutes, whilst the Suffragettes' cunning use of craft turned a typically 'feminine' activity into a form of activism by embroidering banners with their political manifesto. The Suffragettes may have succeeded in gaining the right for women to vote, but as the century progressed these traditional crafts became seen as means of keeping women assigned to traditional roles. The feminists took against crafts with a vengeance, and women who practised needlework were seen as passive victims of a patriarchal hegemony.

In 1984, Roszika Parker published a comprehensive history of embroidery that would challenge this theory. Entitled *Subversive Stitch: Embroidery and the Making of the Feminine*, she details how over the centuries embroidery, rather than

"An embroiderer can become
a sociologist but does not bring
her work out in staffroom,
boardroom or pub."

being a tool of oppression, enabled women to rally against their position within the home. However, as women gained greater independence and freedom, crafting was left behind. As Parker concludes, "an embroiderer can become a sociologist but does not bring her work out in staffroom, boardroom or pub." Crafting just did not fit with the image of empowered women.

The turnaround in the perception of craft began to take shape in the early 1990s, when Martha Stewart reigned supreme as the squeaky clean American queen of stylish household management. Her magazines and television shows were choc full of craft ideas that struck a chord with the public. "I think the renewed interest in crafts can be attributed initially to *Martha Stewart Living* magazine", says impassioned Toronto knitter Hayley Waxberg. "Martha Stewart changed the image of craft, showing a broad audience that crafts can be elegant and pretty—that they don't have to be tacky." Craft was on the move, but calling Martha Stewart punk rock (even though she is a convicted felon) would be a bit of a stretch of the imagination. Luckily, this role was being filled by another movement that developed simultaneously alongside Martha's inexorable rise: Riot Grrrl.

Riot Grrrl was a rock revolution that took seed in Washington DC, orchestrated by groups of angry girls who mixed feminism with punk and gave the two fingers to 'beergutboyrock'. Although the movement was grounded in music, Riot Grrrl bands like Bikini Kill and Bratmobile were concerned with vocalising a do-it-yourself subculture: organising female-centric music festivals, and spreading the word about sexism and violence against women with cut 'n' paste zines. The movement embraced confrontation and political energy and spread quickly to become a global phenomenon. Although Riot Grrrl wilfully tried to remain true to its principals, media exposure and the assimilation of their manifesto by mainstream pop acts (such as the Spice Girls advocating a spurious 'Girl Power'), meant that by the mid-90s it had lost momentum.

In 1995 Martha Stewart appeared on the cover of *New York Magazine* and was described as "the definitive woman of our time" whilst Riot Grrrl was declared dead. But the movement had made its mark on a number of young women, one of whom was Debbie Stoller, Editor in Chief of her own magazine,

> "In 1995 Martha Stewart appeared on the cover of *New York Magazine*, and was described as 'the definitive woman of our time' whilst Riot Grrrl was declared dead."

> "I began seeing women—young women—knitting on the subway. Soon they were everywhere: at coffee shops, on lunch lines, at the movies, even in bars...."

Bust—an intelligent women's publication with a feminist slant. In 1999 Stoller got a bad case of the knitting bug and began writing about the joys of the handicraft she had been taught by her Dutch family, believing that "knitting is part of the same do-it-yourself ethos that spawned zines and mixed tapes". She set up a knitting circle in New York and in true Riot Grrrl style, named the group Stitch and Bitch. It was a defining moment. Craft came flying out of the closet and into the public arena, and the number of knitters under the age of 35 experienced a whopping 400 per cent increase. "I began seeing women —young women—knitting on the subway. Soon they were everywhere: at coffee shops, on lunch lines, at the movies, even in bars", says Stoller.

It wasn't long before knitting clubs were stitching and bitching all over the world. By 2000 it had hit the United Kingdom, when London's nutty, arty knitters Rachael Matthews and Amy Plant started up Cast Off, a "knitting club for boys and girls". They built on the increasingly rock 'n' roll image, advocating drunken knitting, and getting kicked out of the fancy Savoy hotel in the process for their stick wielding antics.

The knitting phenomenon pulled other lost and forgotten crafts along in its wake: embroidery, crochet and sewing were resurrected from their granny-fied status to join the revolution, and a slew of crafting clubs, websites and publications sprung up at a rate of knots (aha!) to facilitate the crafty tidal wave. Debbie Stoller followed up her seminal book of knitting patterns, *Stitch 'N Bitch: The Knitter's Handbook* with *Stitch 'N Bitch Nation* before moving into crochet with *The Happy Hooker*. Other books have ranged from knits and crafts specifically for your dog (there are quite a few of these in fact) to a craftista's wish come true, *Sew U*, where hip New York based designer, Wendy Mullin of Built By Wendy, explains how to make clothes. Whilst *Bust* and even *Elle Girl* have regularly feature crafty ideas, new magazines dedicated to DIY continue to hit the newsstands: *ReadyMade* magazine offers projects suitable for even the most discerning of urban hipsters (going so far as to explain how to make your own bed), *Adorn* magazine just launched it's premier issue, with the tag line "the craft girl's guide to embellishing life" and as I write, a new US-based magazine dedicated to it's namesake, *Craft*, is on the way.

The Internet has also been instrumental in the new craft movement. Craft blogs and online magazines such as *Knitty* and the new *Whip Up* provide craft inspiration free of charge, whilst in 2003 Leah Kramer gave us the mothership of Internet crafting: Craftster.org. Craftster rules that there be "no tea cosies without irony", and is a sprawling forum for the craft community to share ideas, tips and banter. It now has over 55,000 members and boasts over 25,000,000 views per month. Craft is even making it onto the small screen. Vickie Howell, a founding member of the Austin Craft Mafia, is something of a younger, cooler Martha Stewart. She has been presenting *Knitty Gritty* on the DIY Network for a number of seasons and has recently added *Stylelicious* to her repertoire to showcase handmade clothes. The revolution will be televised!

Renegade or Retrograde?

Yet even today Stoller admits that this kind of renegade craft isn't on everyone's radar. As she told *Spun* magazine, "It is a pretty straight-forward idea, but it's hard for people to grasp sometimes. They really have a hard time acknowledging that there is this population that are kind of alternative chicks, who are sort of feminist and crafty and into the indie rock scene. People don't even realize that those people exist."

And some people downright disapprove of it. In her seminal feminist edict, *The Feminine Mystique*, 1968, Betty Friedan saw needlecrafts as a means by which women were kept tied to the drudgery of housewifery, and a number of contemporary feminists seem inclined to agree. Germaine Greer noted in 1999's *The Whole Woman* that, "not all feminists have regarded women's traditional skills with contempt; there are feminists who see the home as a creative opportunity, who bake bread and cakes, who knit and sew, who grow fruit and vegetables and make pickles" (and here comes the sting) "in the forlorn hope that someone will value the work of their hands above the work of machines."

Easy now ladies! What Ms Friedan and Greer didn't anticipate was that handicrafts don't need to be domestic. Crafting groups meeting in bars, parks or on public transport have taken a somewhat solitary act out of the home, whilst Knitta Please have quite literally taken it to the streets. They knit up fabulous

"We've come to a point of modernity where everywhere you look it's just excess, excess, excess.... By making my own clothes I am ensuring that no one is exploited in their creation."

creations and then under the cover of darkness use them to 'graffiti' the city (give it a go yourself on page 104).

Neither do crafters sit around waiting for someone to praise their endeavour. As Stoller explains, "Betty Friedan and other like-minded feminists had overlooked an important aspect of knitting when they viewed it simply as part of a women's societal obligation to serve everyone around them—they had forgotten that knitting served the knitter as well."

The Great Craft Democracy

Since craft is intrinsically involved in feminist discourse, it's easy to forget the men of the movement. Whilst newspapers were harping on about Russell Crowe being a knitter (I'm yet to be convinced), bona fide punk rocker Greg der Ananian was stirring up some serious badass craft mayhem encouraging reprobate crafters to sell their wares at his alterna-craft fair, Bizarre Bazaar. In his book of the same name, his dirty pillow project shows you how to embroider a picture of a slice of cherry pie with the message "tastes so good make a grown man cry": it's a decidedly mild example of his downright filthy cross-stitching.

There is no doubt that the (only slightly) less fair sex can stitch and bitch like any lady, but as Susan Cropper, who owns the knitting boutique Loop, in London, has observed; "some guys come in with their girlfriends or boyfriends and shop to learn to knit. Some take the classes, but I would be lying if I said it was very many. This is a gap for me—I think men are still pretty funny about being seen doing something that has traditionally been seen as a women's craft." Nonetheless, a few groups of guys have managed to overcome their prejudice, and a number of exclusive knitting circles are springing up. And they've got some of the best names around: Dicks with Sticks in San Francisco, Men with Balls in Denver, Colorado, and Stitches in Britches in Chicago.

Just as men are welcomed into the craft fray so is your gran and all her WI mates. Greg Der Ananian may have subtitled his book *Not Your Granny's Craft*, but he explains that despite the distance contemporary craftsters have put between themselves and the fusty old-school perceptions of craft fetes in church halls, the traditional legacy of craft is part of its appeal.

> "... the punk rock aspect of this new craft revolution is that ultimately there is no hierarchy."

In fact he thinks it's a great way for different generations to connect: "I'm a 31 year old gay man in LA and my mom's a 64 year old housewife in suburbia—at the same time we both love cross-stitching and knitting, so we can talk about that. Granted we do really different things with them, but it's still really cool." The outlaw knitting graffiti crew, Knitta Please, has a 70-year-old granny amongst its ranks and as Betsy Greer sees it, "the punk rock aspect of this new craft revolution is that ultimately there is no hierarchy". Cast Off's constitution states this position clearly: "anyone, regardless of age, cultural background, gender, disability and health status is welcome".

Now Get Your Craft On!

So you've been invited to the party, but do you have the courage to dance?

The biggest boundary to an all-inclusive craft nation is that people feel they need to be naturally creative to make stuff. Take a moment to think about Berlin nutters, Chicks On Speed. One of their early mantras was the irreverent "Fuck Art, Let's Craft", and they managed to be a band without knowing anything about music. They may sing, "We like using gaffer tape, but we don't play guitar", but they have three record labels and travel the world as musicians, fashion designers and artists—all in the spirit of DIY.

So slip into a pair of overalls (this seems to help the Chicks On Speed) and get to it. After all, the crafty ladies and gentlemen behind *Making Stuff* don't want you to admire their handiwork —they want to encourage you to craft up your own. That's right, I said do it yourself—quite frankly, it would be rude not to! If all fails, break out the gaffer tape. And if you need any more reasons to craft, here's just a few:

Craft for Craft's Sake: Reasons to Craft

Before the industrial revolution, making stuff was a way of life because daily necessities like clothes were not readily available to buy. Today however, anti-consumerism has played a big part in the resurgence of DIY. In 2005 the Portland, Oregon-based group Super Crafty brought out their eponymous craft book with the tagline, "Saving the World from Mass Production". Just like punk rock, craft is embedded in an anti-establishment/anti-

consumerist ethos and as the ever-quotable Betsy Greer reminds us, "being able to make your own clothes and accessories from scratch is punk as fuck." She goes on to explain; "we've come to a point of modernity where everywhere you look it's just excess, excess, excess.... By making my own clothes I am ensuring that no one is exploited in their creation. Unless I make my clothes from yarn from my own sheep, I am still purchasing materials for crafts, but in starting to think about clothes as something you have the choice to design, you are taking a step back from materialism."

As well as being socially beneficial, many crafters will sing the praises of knitting, crochet, embroidery, etc., as a great means of unwinding (!), such as Hayley Waxberg, who says, "My health suffers if I'm not making something everyday. I find it very meditative, it seems to lower my stress levels and improves my patience and outlook." And Camilla Stacey deliberately sticks strictly to stress-busting tasks: "I find knitting really calms you down, and all I have done is knit scarves. I have absolutely no interest in making jumpers as the thought of following a pattern stresses me out." The business man John Naisbitt puts a more scientific spin on this meditative aspect of craft with his theory, 'high tech/high touch' which claims that the longer we sit at a computer each day "the more high touch and sensual our leisure activities become (gardening, cooking, carpentry, bird watching)". Or knitting, cross-stitching, jewellery-making and felting.

For some, craft even has a spiritual element (this is where the knitting as the new yoga bit comes in). In 2000 Tristy Taylor and Callie Janoff thought up The Church of Craft in order to promote "any and all acts of creation as a means to live life best". They meet up on a Sunday and supply their congregation with creative inspiration: "The power of creating gives us the confidence to live our lives with all the love we can. By promoting creativity, we offer access to a non-denominational spiritual practice that is self-determined and proactive."

And from spiritual to material—my own personal favourite reason to craft: cheap chic. I don't mind telling you that in recent years my handiness has sprung from a deep desire for things (namely clothes) rather than spirituality. Coupled with an inherent thriftiness, I enjoy the challenge of making my own designs —even if I do need a bit of inspiration from the high street.

"There are tons of overpriced items to be found that people with more money than sense will snap up if there's a brand name slapped on it. Turn it upside down, inside out and work out how it's made. Deconstruct it to reconstruct it."

"Try different materials, different shapes, let your mind branch off in different directions...."

The way to do it is to tackle designer stores and expensive boutiques (or net-a-porter.com for the less daring), but remember some clothes have a high price tag for a reason. Intricate patterns, clever cuts and heavenly fabric are simply beyond the regular crafty diva's skills, but there are tons of overpriced items to be found that people with more money than sense will snap up if there's a brand name slapped on it. Turn it upside down, inside out and work out how it's made. Deconstruct it to reconstruct it. For example, a Mulberry dress I recently spied in a magazine boasting a macramé (and I admit I had previously denounced this hippyish craft) neckline and a £595 price tag inspired me to knock up my own version for about one per cent of the cost—a bit like a one-woman version of Primark, only more ethical. Put it this way, the more clothes you can make on the cheap, the more shoes you can afford to buy to go with them!

Craft Nation

In their fourth issue of *Pamphlet*, indie aficionados and feminist zine scribblers Phoebe Frangoul and Anna Marie expressed the feeling of loss experienced when a niche scene goes global: "the mainstream has swallowed hipster style so absolutely that there's no longer any distinction between mainstream and alternative people. This sucks—I feel like my identity has been stolen and I can't figure out how to assert my individuality through dress any more. This is all Topshop's fault."

Just as the Arts and Crafts movement at the end of the nineteenth century strove to restore the value of handmade goods at a time of industrial revolution, today we are surrounded by mass produced goods yet yearn for something more individual. It is this insatiable quest for a distinct identity that will ensure that the trend for making stuff is only going to grow. And unlike when everyone shops at one high street shop, no matter how many people start making things, no two people will create exactly the same 'look' because each handcrafted item will be individual from the next, and so will each crafter. There will be mother earth crafters, rebel crafters, immaculate crafters (how do they keep their nails so neat?), messy crafters, drunken crafters, teetotal crafters, high-fashion crafters, thrifty crafters and luxury crafters. Really anyone can make stuff, and it's probably only a matter of time before they do.

When we decided to put this book together, we put out an open call to people all over the United Kingdom. The response was phenomenal. Amateurs and professionals, young and old came out of the woodwork, with brilliant, fascinating and downright bizarre ideas for things to make and do. The word seemed to spread like wildfire, and we found that people in Canada, the United States and Scandinavia were writing in as well. We couldn't include all of them, but we chose the ones we liked best, and I hope you like them too. Most of them are pretty straightforward, with a few more complex ideas for the advanced craftster. All of them are open to interpretation, and one of the things the contributors to this book kept emphasising was: "do it your own way". Try different materials, different shapes, let your mind branch off in different directions. Use this book as you would a cookbook. You can follow the instructions, or you can use the combinations of flavours as pure inspiration....

Be warned! Hardened craftistas refer to 'getting the craft bug' —once you're in it's hard to get out... even my craft-bashing friend Katy has now got her two feet firmly in the craft camp and unashamedly sings the praises of a spot of felting (see her amazing flowers on page 92). If you've already got the bug then the only path of action is to get your own crafting circle going to recruit yet more to the cause. Draw up your own craft manifesto and cause a riot, the words of the anarchist feminist and troublemaker, Emma Goldman are a good place to start: "If I can't dance I don't want to be in your revolution."

Welcome to the dancefloor.

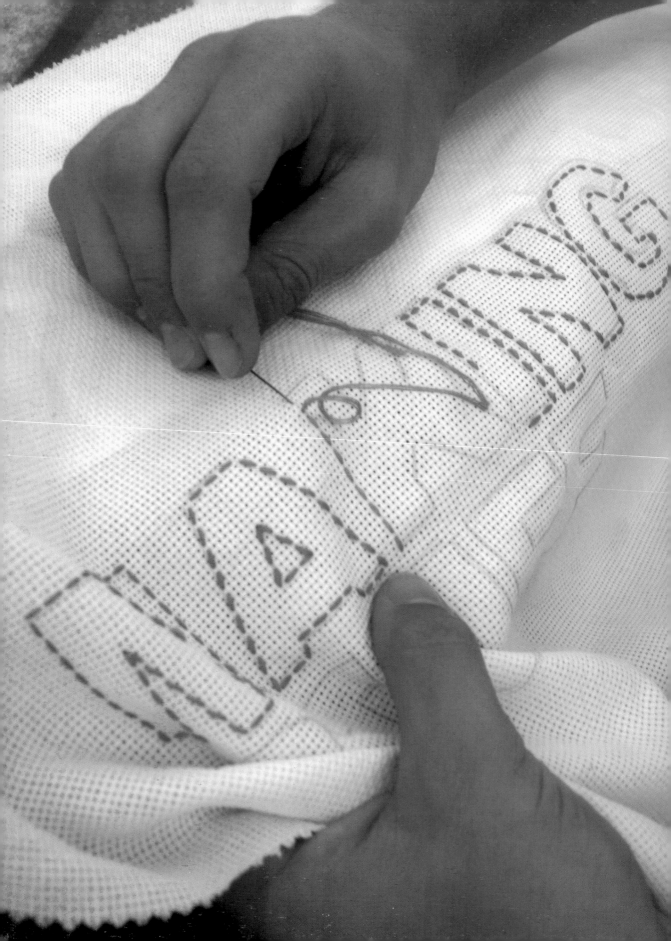

HOW TO...

The ancient technique of looping bits of string together with a couple of sticks has never been so vibrant. With hip patterns abounding and beautiful yarns stocking the shelves of hip knit shops, it has well and truly dropped it's fuddy-duddy image. For the novice knitter, it can all seem a little bit overwhelming at first, but as Susan Cropper of the London knitting boutique Loop explains, the key is "not to be afraid to make mistakes… You have to remember, it's just yarn, and it can be pulled out and started again…."

Really anyone can do it. Burly punk rocker and craft author Greg Der Ananian doesn't let his hefty hands get in the way of his knit: "You need some fine motor control skill. Everyone who learns to knit takes a little while to find their groove—your stitches might be kind of uneven at first—but with a little perseverance you can become a skilled knitter. Put in a little time and engage in the repetition that will give your hands the muscle memory to do the necessary things."

And without further ado, here's what you do.

The Knit Kit

Sticks

Knitting needles are made in a variety of materials—metal, plastic, bamboo and wood are the most common ones. You can also get different lengths and thicknesses. The longer the needles, the more stitches you can fit on. So if you are knitting something big—like a jumper—you need a longer length. All the projects in this book are fairly small, so the length doesn't matter, but you do need to pay attention to the width. In the UK this is measured in mm (and by a different point system in the US, so be careful) and is referred to as the needle size. The size you use depends upon the thickness of your yarn.

String

Basically, you can knit with any long string, the most common being balls of yarn. The label will tell you everything you need to know about your yarn; what the fibre is made of (wool, cotton, acrylic, etc.) and also tell you what size needles to use and what your gauge will be—don't freak out just yet! Forget about your gauge for a moment—just make sure that your sticks and string are compatible.

Things

Scissors, pins and a measuring tape will come in handy and a yarn needle (a big chunky sewing needle with a blunt tip) is indispensable. Stitch markers are useful and so is a row counter. You may also require a stitch holder—they do as their name suggests and look like big safety pins.

Getting Started

There are a couple of things you need to get to grips with before you can start to knit.

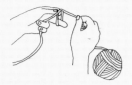  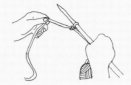

Slip-knot

1. Take a length of yarn about 30 cm along and make a small loop, crossing over the yarn from the tail and the yarn that connects to the ball. Hold the point where they cross between your fingers.

2. With your spare hand, stick a finger through the loop, hook the yarn attached to the ball and bring it through the circle, forming a new loop. Keep hold of this loop and let go of the original circle.

3. Pull the tail end tight to form a knot at the bottom of the loop. Push a needle through the loop and pull both yarns so that the knot slips to the size of the needle.

Double Cast On (aka long tail cast on)

The slip-knot is the first loop and now you just need a few more. There are various ways to do this but the double cast on is a universal favourite as it's nice and stretchy. You need a long tail to do this. How long depends on the number of stitches you need to cast on—for now 30 cm will do, but in the future, multiply the number of stitches you need to cast on by three and then add another 20 cm for good measure—always overestimate. This is a bit tricky, so read carefully.

1. Hold the needle with the slip-knot on it in your right hand. Hold the two yarns apart by wrapping the tail end of the yarn around your left thumb and the yarn attached to the ball over your index finger. Keep the remainder of the yarn out of the way by covering it in your palm with your remaining left hand fingers.

2. Place the tip of the needle under the yarn that runs from palm to thumb and pick it up.

3. Make sure this yarn stays on the needle (pop a finger on top of it if you need to) then dip the needle under the yarn that runs from the index finger to the needle, moving the needle towards your thumb and bring it through the space you will see between the two yarns to the thumb.

4. Move your thumb out of the loop and pull on the tail to tighten the stitch (don't pull so tight that the yarn is stretched, or your first row of knitting will be really awkward). Repeat until you have as many stitches as you need.

This Is Knit

Knitting basically involves pulling one loop through another. Before you attempt to knit a 'thing', gather together your sticks and string and just practise.

1. Hold the needle with the cast on stitches on it in your left hand and the empty needle in your right. The yarn also goes in your right hand (try weaving it between your fingers to keep hold of it) behind the needles. Stick the tip of the right hand needle into the first loop, from left to right.

2. Bring the yarn over the point of the right hand needle in a clockwise motion, using your index finger. To steady the motion, grip the two needles between the thumb and index finger on your left hand whilst your right hand wraps the yarn.

3. Take control of the right needle again and bring it back out of the loop you pushed it into. Easy enough, except you need to pull the yarn that is over the tip back through the loop with it. You now have a loop on the right hand needle.

4. Push the right hand needle a little further through the loop and move it over to the right so that the original loop slides off the tip of the left needle. This makes one whole stitch.

5. Repeat steps 1–4 for each stitch on the row. At the end of the row, switch your needle from one hand to the other and begin again on the other side of the fabric.

Purl-y Queen

A knit stitch looks like a V on the front of the fabric and a bump on the back, so sometimes you want to do a backwards knit stitch to get a bump on the front and a V on the back. A back-to-front knit stitch is called a purl.

1. Hold the needle with all the stitches on it in your left hand as with knitting, but keep the yarn in front of the needles. Insert the tip of the right hand needle into the first loop, from back to front and right to left.

2. Bring the yarn over the tip of the needle in an anti-clockwise motion, pulling it back round in front of the needles.

3. Bring the right hand needle back out of the stitch, making sure that you bring the yarn wrapped over it back through the loop with the needle. You now have a new loop on the right hand needle.

4. Just like for the knit stitch, push the right hand needle a little further through the new loop. Move the right hand needle to the right to pull the original loop off the left needle and leave a new one on the right. Repeat steps 1–4 for each stitch on the row.

A Stitch Mix

By using different mixes of stitches you get different effects. The main ones are:

Garter stitch
Knit every row. It has a bumpy effect and makes a great first scarf.

Stockinette stitch
Knit one row, purl one row. The majority of knit clothes use this. You get all the 'V's on one side and all the bumps on the other. It is no good for making a scarf as the edges tend to curl up.

Rib
Knit one stitch, purl one stitch, knit one stitch, etc.. To switch from knit to purl like this you have to move the yarn between the needle tips from the back to the front. You can also knit two, purl two and other variations.

Cast Off

So you know how to knit, purl and combine the two. The world is your lobster, right? Almost. You need to seal off your knitting, otherwise the whole darn thing is going to unwind. Sometimes referred to as 'binding off', casting off is basically securing the 'live' loops on the needle. Don't worry, it's much easier than casting on!

1. Knit the first two stitches on the row as normal.

2. Then insert the left hand needle into the first stitch on the right hand needle. Lift it over the first stitch and off the end of the needle. Let go of the stitch—it has now been cast off.

3. Knit another stitch as normal and again lift the first stitch on the right hand needle over the new stitch and the end of the needle.

4. Repeat step 3 until you only have one stitch left on the left hand needle. Cut the yarn with about 15 cm spare, push the end through the loop and pull tight.

5. Think you've finished? To be done and dusted you must weave in all the 15 cm tails. All you do is thread the end through a yarn needle and on the back of the knit fabric pass the needle under the stitches until you can't go any further. Snip off the yarn close to the knit.

Your Gauge Does Matter!

Gauge is the number of rows and/or stitches per length/width of a knitted fabric. It is what you use to check that you are knitting to the same tension as the person who constructed the pattern. This is less important when knitting something like a scarf, where the width and length won't alter the fit, but with large items like jumpers, the size of the final product is fairly crucial.

Work out if you are tight or loose!

Some people knit tightly and others loosely. Before you begin a project, knit up a test square to check which size needles you need to knit to the tension demanded in the pattern. So, if you're a loose knitter you may need smaller needles than suggested, where as a wound-up tight knitter may need larger needles.

1. Cast on 20–40 stitches (depending on the thickness of the yarn you're using—look at the label and cast on the amount it tells you the gauge will be and six or so more) and knit until you have a square in stockinette stitch (knit one row, purl one row).

2. Count the rows and stitches in a 10 × 10 cm area. A good way to do this is to take one side of a cereal packet, and cut out a 10 cm square. Place it over the fabric and count.

3. If it is the same as the count required by the pattern then off you go! However, if you have fewer than the required count you need to do another swatch with bigger needles. If your count is too high then go down one size. Keep going until you get it right. This may seem tedious, but it is better than slaving over a project only to find out that it doesn't fit!

You can play around with the tension to get different effects. So, for the i-Pod cosy (see page 100), which uses worsted weight yarn, you would normally use 4–5 mm needles, but by using a slightly smaller set of 3.5 mm needles, the stitches are smaller and this results in a thicker, sturdier fabric.

From One Ball To Another

When you finish one ball of yarn, you need to begin with another, and you'll often also want to change colour to make stripes. The best place to do this is at the end of a row.

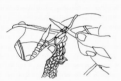  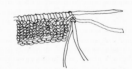

1. Cut the yarn leaving a 15 cm tail and place the beginning of the new ball of yarn with the tail. Hold them tightly together in your left hand.

2. Knit six stitches using the new yarn, keeping hold of both yarns in your left hand.

3. Stop for a moment and knot the two tails together firmly (but not too tight as you will undo it later).

4. Carry on knitting (and purling!). When your knit is complete you can undo the joining knots and weave in all the ends to secure—this will give a bump free finish.

What It All Means

So now you know how to knit, and you're itching to start on a pattern. But what do all those letters mean?

co	Cast on	tog	Together
k	Knit	dec	Decrease
p	Purl	inc	Increase
st(s)	Stitch(es)	bo	Bind off/Cast off
sl	Slip		
psso	Pass slipped stitch over		
m1	Make 1 increase		

When you see an *, this denotes a series of steps that are repeated either a specified number of times or all the way across the row.

You've mastered the basics for a single, rectangular piece of knitting, but for slightly more complicated patterns, you'll want to join two or more pieces together and add some shaping. Here's how:

Mattress Stitch

The Mattress Stitch is the best way to join two side seams together. You'll need a yarn needle and a long length of the same yarn that you knitted with.

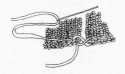

1. Place the two seams you want to join together and pin into place. Attach the yarn to the bottom corner of the right hand piece by bringing the needle through from the wrong side to the right (leave a 15 cm tail to weave in afterwards) and then take the needle over the edge of the fabric and push up from wrong side to right again. Pull tight—you're attached!

2. Now pull the other corner in. Push the needle through the corner stitch and the left hand piece from the right side to the wrong side. And once more, on the right side, up from the wrong side to the right. Confusing? Really it isn't—it's like a figure of 8—and it doesn't matter what you do so long as the corners are together.

3. With the right sides facing you, use your fingers to pull the lumpy, bumpy edge away from the knit piece (it helps if you have a bit longer nails—sorry boys!) As you can see, there is a ladder of horizontal bars.

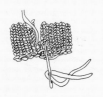

4. All you do is push the needle under two of the bars on one side…

5. … and then under two bars on the other side.

6. Carry on in this way all along the seams, always from one side to the other. Pull tight and the stitches will… disappear.

   Finish by doing the figure of 8 thing again!

Back Stitch

After the mattress stitch, the backstitch is a piece of cake! It is a good join to use on two cast on edges. It is a bit bulky, but also strong and sturdy.

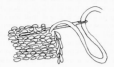 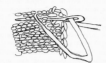

1. Place the right sides together and pin matching up the rows. Work at least one stitch in from the edges and make a stitch through both layers about 1 cm long. Pull the thread through.

2. Now track back (hence the name), push the needle through the fabric midway between where you pushed the needle in and where it emerged on the last stitch. Make another 1 cm stitch, bringing the needle up about 0.5 cm further along than last time.

3. Repeat step 2 until you are done.

You'd Better Shape Up

A common mistake of new knitters is to increase and decrease the number of stitches by mistake, by dropping stitches and losing count on rows. The knit knowledge you have so far will give you rectangles (perfect for scarves and antennae cosies), but to make any other shapes you need to add a few more tricks to your sticks, and increase and decrease the number of stitches —on purpose.

Increasing

There are a few ways to do this, but for the purposes of this book, here is an easy little number to make an extra stitch.

1. So, if the pattern reads k5, m1, k5, knit five stitches and at this point instead of inserting the needle into the next loop, place the tip of the right hand needle under the bar between the two stitches, from front to back.

2. Transfer this loop to the left hand needle by inserting the tip of the left hand needle under the yarn, from front to back

3. Remove the right hand needle from the loop so that it sits on the left hand needle ready to be knit as normal.

4. Except, you don't knit it quite as normal! You knit into the back of the stitch. You may need to pull the back part of the loop away from the needle with your fingers to insert the tip of the right hand needle into it from right to left. Wrap the yarn as normal. An extra stitch! Continue to knit the next five stitches normally.

Decreasing

Here are two ways to decrease for you to try your hand at—and they won't leave a hole. They slant in different ways so you will probably use a different method on either side of your knit piece. In this book we tell you which type to use.

Knit 2 Together
Slants to the right (k2tog)

Slip, Knit, Pass Slipped Stitch Over
Slants to the left

1. This is ridiculously easy. All you do is carry out a knit stitch in exactly the same way as usual—just insert the needle through two loops instead of one.

1. To slip a stitch all you do is stick the right hand needle as if you are going to knit it—but don't! Just remove the left hand needle, passing it onto the right hand needle.

2. Knit the next stitch as normal.

3. With the left hand needle, pick up the slipped stitch and pull it over the knit stitch and the tip of the right hand needle (like you do when casting off).

Slip Stitch on it's own: sometimes you need to slip a stitch without the rest of the decrease manoeuvre—just follow step 1—that's it!

Buttonhole

Basically a buttonhole is made by casting off a number of stitches in the middle of a row and then casting them back on the row above.

1. The pattern will tell you where to cast off the stitches. Note that you will knit the required amount and then 2 more, because these are the ones that will be cast off. So if the pattern reads: k5, co3, you knit five and then knit two more. Return and pull the first extra stitch over the second and off the needle. Cast off the amount required, then you will have a stitch on the right hand needle (this is included in the remainder of knit stitches, so if after co3 the pattern tells you to k5, you count this one and knit four more)—just add to it by knitting as usual to the end of the row.

2. On the next row knit (or purl as required) up to the gap where you cast off the stitches. Swap the needles to the opposite hands, and cast on the same number of stitches you cast off, working left to right for a change. You can't use the double cast on method as you only have the length of ball from the yarn. Instead use the cable cast on.

Cable Cast On In The Middle Of A Row

1. Having switched over your needles, knit a stitch in the normal way but don't slip the original stitch off the left hand needle.

2. Now take the new stitch and put it onto the left hand needle next to the original stitch. To do this push the tip of the left hand needle into the front of the loop from left to right, and remove the right hand needle. You've cast on one stitch.

3. To cast on more stitches, point the right hand needle through the space between the first two stitches. Wrap the yarn over the needle as you do with a regular knit stitch and pull it through onto the right hand needle. Pass the loop over to the right hand needle as before.

4. Cast on as many as required. A tip to make it neat is to bring the yarn from the back to the front of your work as you cast on the last stitch, after making the stitch and before transferring it to the left hand needle. Now switch hands again, and (thank heavens!) go back to knitting right to left.

Duplicate Stitch: Two Stitches For The Price Of One

Yet more sewing for knitters—the duplicate stitch is a cunning way to add images to knitting after it is knitted! You can work patterns in as you go using a technique called intarsia, but this looks just as good and is much less complicated.

1. With your trusty yarn needle, thread a length of yarn. Use the same type of yarn as you used to knit, just a different colour of course, or it won't show up! Work out where your image is going, and attach the yarn at the back of the piece. Work from the bottom of the image. Choose your first stitch and bring the needle through to the front at the bottom of the 'V'. Pull the yarn all the way through.

2. Now thread the needle under the two 'V' legs of the stitch above and pull the yarn through.

3. Finally, take the needle back through the hole at the bottom of the 'V' that the needle came up through.

4. Repeat on the next stitch. It is easiest to work across one row, then along the row above, and so on.

In Addition

There is not much more you need to know. If you have any problems, the Internet is an invaluable source of knit know-how (see the directory at the back of this book). Once you've got it mastered, you can spend some time on the finishing touches. Susan Cropper recommends you "have fun embellishing the simplest scarf pattern by adding clusters of buttons, pom-poms, fringe or ribbon".

HOW TO... FELT

Felting is one of the easiest crafts to master, and the results are astoundingly effective. Get an old jumper, stick it in the washing machine on a hot wash, take it out, and the result is a very dense, exceptionally warm material that will not fray when you cut it.

In this book you will find instructions for making felted mittens, tea cosies and felted flowers, but the joy of felt is that you can use it for just about anything—hats, scarves, bags, cuddly toys, baby booties... the possibilities are endless, and all you need is that simple, unforgettable equation: wool + hot water = felt.

Here's how to do it

1. Find a jumper or a scarf that you don't want any more, and check the garment label to make sure it is wool. Only pure wool will be suitable for shrinking or "fulling" in a washing machine. Occasionally mixed wool garments, e.g. 80% wool 20% nylon, will work. Check the label—if it says handwash only, it should felt.

2. Lay the garment out and measure.

3. Place the garment in the washing machine, add 2 or 3 tbsp. of delicate wool wash detergent and select hot wash.

4. If you are using a pure wool garment (such as lambswool), wash at 60° Celsius. Washing at a higher temperature may make the fabric too dense to sew easily. If it's a nylon mix, you can try at 70°. Angora and mohair felt very easily, so you might want to try a lower temperature first.

5. When the cycle has ended, remove the woollen piece and measure it again to check how much shrinkage has occurred. The maximum shrinkage you should be looking for is 50%. Anywhere from 20° to 40° is desirable (depending on the texture that you're after). If it has shrunk successfully, then it is ready for use. If it has not shrunk much, then repeat the washing at a higher temperature.

6. Allow the garment to dry. Once fully dry you will be able to cut the fabric without the edges fraying.

Tips

+ Merino wool will not felt, as it is usually machine washable.

+ Hand knitted garments tend to shrink more than shop bought ones.

+ These instructions are for machine felting. If you are working with wool fleece rather than pre-knitted garments, hand felting will be required. This is a very similar method, but involves soaking, soaping and agitating the wool fibres by hand.

How to recycle a sweater/jumper into a multitude of household & personal accessories!!

mittens x 1 pair
leftovers-stuffing
tea cozy x 1
Hot water bottle covers x 2
scarves x 2 or 3

+ crewnecks best, but v-necks also work

+ Look for 100% wool, 100% lambswool

+ grody colours you wouldn't want to wear can turn out fantastic when embellished

+ the bigger the jumper the more fabric so go for XXL

+ patterns can be great and can require less embellishment—great for those last minute gifts

+ can all be handsewn, though a sewing machine will speed up the work

+ start with a clean, dry jumper so there's no shrinkage in your final product after washing

HOW TO... APPLIQUÉ

Appliqué is a sewing technique where fabric shapes are attached onto a base fabric. You are supposed to turn under the edges of your fabric shape for a neat look, but if you use felt or t-shirt fabric (iron on some interfacing to make it a bit stiffer) there is no need to do this.

1. Draw the image onto the felt or t-shirt material.

2. Cut out, dab with glue, and position them on your work.

3. Now stitch into place. Use thread that matches the colour of the appliqué shape. Push the needle through the base fabric and bring it up through the appliqué fabric. Pull tight and repeat all the way around the edge, in a simple overhand stitch.

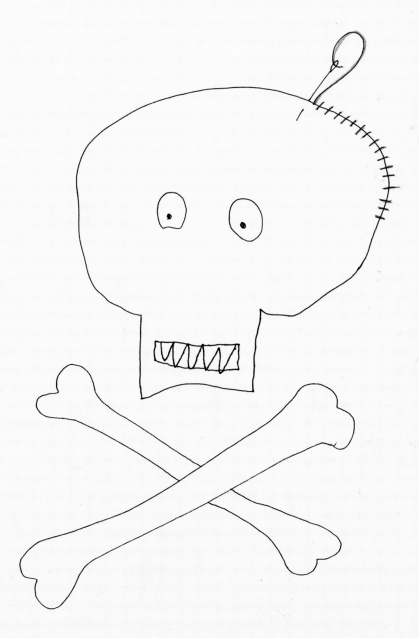

Sewing is a basic skill that every craftster needs to know. Two bits of fabric, a needle and some thread is all you need. Of course a sewing machine always helps, and is in some cases essential, such as when fabric is too thick to join together (this can often happen when working with felted wool). Sewing machines are not expensive (a basic one costs around £100/$180), and purchasing one is certainly recommended. If you do choose to buy one, try and get a demonstration from the shop assistant of how to thread it—although this is usually fairly coherently explained in the manual.

There are some things, however, that a standard sewing machine can't achieve. When you're actively seeking a rough and rugged look; when you're embarking on basic embroidery stitches; or when you just want to show off your fancy sewing skills, for example. There are countless stitches that an avid seamster/ess can learn. Here are some of the basics:

Straight or Running Stitch
This is the standard broken-dash stitch. Just run your needle in and out through the fabric, in a linear fashion. Make sure to knot your thread or to sew a couple small stitches one on top of the other before starting and after finishing your seam, so it doesn't unravel (this is called a back stitch).

Basting Stitch
Exactly the same as the running stitch, except that the lengths of the stitches are exceptionally long. This is used to hold two pieces of fabric in place before running them through the sewing machine.

Split Stitch
This stitch creates a continuous running line, with no breaks at all. It's good for basic embroidery, as you can use it to follow any line drawing you like.

All you need to do, is make a small stitch, and then bring the needle up for the next stitch through the centre of the thread of the previous stitch, 'splitting' it.

Blanket Stitch
This utilitarian and aesthetically pleasing stitch can be used along the edge of your fabric, to make visible chunky stitches in a contrasting colour.

Work from left to right. Bring the needle up from the wrong side of the fabric, make a diagonal stitch, and when you bring your needle up to make the next stitch, come up under the first one, pulling the thread down to make a right angle.

Whip Stitch

This little number joins two edges on the right sides of the fabric.

Join the thread onto the fabric and hold the fabric with one hand. Pass the needle from one side to the other. Bring the needle over the top of the join and pass the needle through the fabric in the same direction as before.

Chain Stitch

Pull your thread up through the fabric and reinsert next to where the needle just exited. Instead of pulling the thread through into a stitch, leave the thread in a loose loop. Bring your needle up under this loop and through it to make your next stitch. The result is a continuous stitch that can look a little like the split stitch.

CRUCIAL MEASUREMENTS

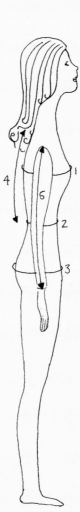

1. Bust
2. Waist
3. Hips
4. Back-waist length
5. Sleeve length
6. Back width

HOW TO... CROCHET

The word 'crochet' comes from the French word 'croche', meaning 'hook', and indeed all you need to crochet is a single crochet hook and a ball of yarn. The concept is very simple—it's a series of loops that are secured when the free end of the thread is pulled through the final loop. The result is a very versatile craft. By combining basic crochet stitches and lighter weight or softer yarns, you can create a soft, drapable material, a bit like knitted fabric, that works well for clothing and accessories. A thicker yarn, more densely stitched, produces a very sturdy, relatively stiff material that is good for durable home accessories. As with any new skill, crochet requires a degree of patience and perseverance, but keep at it.... It's fun, relaxing and very rewarding. Crochet is the new knitting!

1. Hold your crochet hook in your right hand as if you're holding a pencil, and make a slipknot around it, about 10 cm before the end of the yarn.

2. With your left index finger, bring your yarn over the crochet hook from back to front and grab it with the hook.

3. With the hook, pull the yarn through the slipknot and onto the hook. This makes one chain stitch.

4. Skipping the first chain stitch, insert the hook into the centre of the next chain's stitch. Draw the yarn through the chain stitch and up onto the hook. There are now two loops on the hook.

5. Bring the yarn over the hook from back to front and draw it through both loops on the hook. One loop remains on the hook, you can pat yourself on the back for completing your first single chain stitch.

6. Make as many chains as your pattern calls for. Do not count the slipknot or the loop currently on your hook as chain stitches.

7. At the end of the row, make one chain stitch and then turn the work counter clockwise, leaving the hook in the chain. This is called 'turning'.

8. Now begin another row, using the previous row as the knots. When you get to the end, be sure to work your yarn into the last stitch. (If you find that the item you're making gets narrower as you go along, you are probably missing crocheting in the last stitch of each row—a common beginner mistake.)

9. Keep going as your pattern requires.

10. To finish the piece, cut the yarn, 10 cm from the end of your crocheted fabric. Draw the hook straight up, bringing the yarn through the remaining loop on the hook.

11. Take a large yarn needle (you may have one from your adventures in knitting), and thread the yarn into it. Weave it through the stitches to secure.

The Double Crochet Stitch

Double crochet, like the single crochet, builds on a foundation chain as a base. However, as the double crochet works off the extra loops it has an extra height to it.

remaining 2 loops

1. Make a foundation chain of 14 stitches for a practice swatch of 12 stitches. Holding the foundation chain with the front facing you, bring the yarn over and put the hook into the fourth chain from the hook.

2. Bring the yarn over again, and draw the hook and yarn through the chain. There should be three loops on the hook.

3. Yarn over again and pull the hook through the first two loops.

4. Yarn over again and pull the hook through the remaining two loops.

5. Well done! You have just completed one double crochet stitch. Continue to work across the row, making one double crochet in each chain stitch.

6. At the end of the row, you should have 12 stitches, if you count the three chains you skipped at the beginning of the row as a single stitch.

7. Chain 3, turn. This turning chain will be counted as the first stitch of the next row.

8. For further rows: Yarn over and insert your hook into the second stitch. Now work a double crochet.

9. Keep going across the row. Work the final stitch of the row into the turning chain of the previous row. Insert the hook into the top chain.

10. Since you count the turning chain as a stitch in double crochet, you should make a stitch in it. Count your stitches. You should still have 12. Chain 3 and turn to continue.

MADE TO MEASURE

CLOTHING FOR THE DISCERNING CRAFTSTER

+ Get Felt Up Mittens
+ Sew Pretty Pinny
+ Wings of Desire
+ The 'Tie It Up' Top
+ Unicorn Believer
+ Ra Ra Apron
+ Skinny Ribbing Scarf
+ Bow Down Belt
+ Eco Shopper

GET FELT UP MITTENS

Warm hands are only a wash away! These cosy mitts started life as a Marks & Spencer jumper... oops. Lazy guys and girls will know this story all too well: when the label says 'hand wash', what do you do? Bung it in the machine of course. But all is not lost, you can turn the shrunken item into a stylish and oh-so-soft pair of mittens.

Materials

+ 1 old jumper
+ 2 A4 sheets of paper (or US Letter)
+ Dressmaker's pins
+ Needle and thread

Instructions

1. If you haven't got a pre-felted misshapen jumper (well done —you've been doing your hand washing!) you need to make one. See page 24 for how you can do this in a washing machine, and leave it to dry.

2. Draw around your hand on a piece of paper (or whoever's hands the mitts will be warming) with your thumb out to the side (where it sits naturally when you place your hand on a flat surface).

3. Draw the mitten shape around the handprint—.5 cm bigger all the way around. Curve the top evenly and symmetrically. Don't make the wrist area too small as you have to fit your hand through here and felt won't stretch very much. If it ends up too big you can always make it smaller.

4. Cut out and make an identical template.

5. Once your jumper is dry, give it a quick iron, and lay it out on a flat surface. Make sure the two sides of the jumper are lying directly on top of one another.

6. Place the mitten templates on the jumper with the wrists on the waistband; the ribbing will create a stylish detail! Pin the templates onto the jumper. Cut alongside the template (fig. 1). You need a really good pair of scissors to hack through two layers of felt.

7. Remove the templates. If you want to do any stitchery on the front of your mittens, do it now—it'll be much easier than when they are sewn together. You can decorate the left mitten with an 'L' using a simple running stitch in knitting yarn. You could also do a bit of appliqué (see page 25).

8. Pin the two felt layers together again, and sew around the mitts, a few millimetres from the edge. You can do this on a machine or by hand with a running stitch—don't sew up the cuff! The seam will stay on the outside of the mittens, so if you want to make a feature of it, you could opt for chunky yarn and use a blanket stitch (fig. 2).

9. Since you don't want to lose these babies, make like a mum and put them on a string through your coat. To do this, cut a long strip from the jumper by cutting up the arm, under the neck band and down the other arm and attach the ends with a couple of stitches to the inside of the wrist on both mitts. Alternatively, use ribbon and they will look as good hanging off your wrists as on your hands.

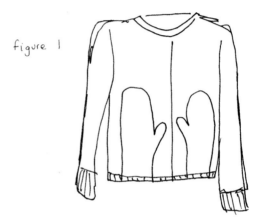

figure 1

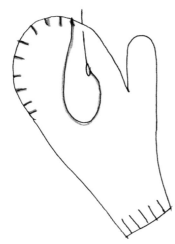

figure 2

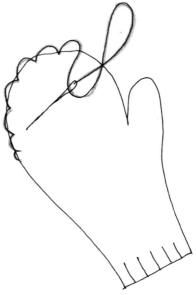

Ruth Singer

SEW PRETTY PINNY

This pinny may indeed be pretty, but with big pockets you can use it for far more than stashing your pin money. You don't have to be a domestic goddess to wear an apron—use it when you're making a creative mess to keep paintbrushes and tools close to hand.

Materials

+ 1 main piece of medium weight cotton fabric, 50 × 50 cm
+ 1 piece of medium weight backing fabric, 50 × 50 cm, in a contrasting colour
+ 2 m Grosgrain ribbon or cotton tape, at least 3 cm wide
+ 1 m bias binding, to match or contrast with your main fabric
+ Soft pencil or tailors' chalk
+ Sewing machine or needle and thread

Instructions

1. Enlarge the pattern pieces to the dimensions specified, and cut out. You will need to use A3 paper to get the right size.

2. Fold the fabric and the backing fabric in half, right sides together. Lay the pattern pieces on fabric with arrows on the folded edge. Pin and cut out neatly. Mark all the information from the pattern onto the reverse of the fabric, using tailors' chalk or soft pencil.

3. Take 12 cm of bias binding and fold it in half lengthways. Press with a hot iron. Slot this over the edge of the backing fabric where marked on the pattern. Pin carefully and sew through all layers. Repeat on the other side.

4. Add bias binding to the curved pocket edges of the main piece. To make this easier, set a curve into the binding first, using 35 cm for each side. Fold the bias binding in half lengthways and using the iron, curve the bias binding in the same shape as the pocket (use the pattern piece as a guide). Make sure the fold is at the top edge as you iron it, so the curved bias will fit over the raw edge of the fabric. Stitch this on in the same way as before, and repeat on the other side.

5. Assemble the main and backing pieces. Lay them right sides together with the main fabric on top. Stitch around the apron, using a 1.5 cm seam allowance, and going slowly and carefully on the curves. Using a zigzag stitch, you can overstitch the raw edges if your fabric looks like it might fray. Notch the curved seams by cutting out small V-shapes, to help it sit flat. Don't cut the notches too close to the stitching.

6. Turn the apron the right way around and iron it neatly, ensuring the curved seam is turned out fully. At the top of the apron, pin the centre of the main fabric onto the centre of the backing fabric. Stitch down the centre of the apron to make two pockets. This stitching will stop the apron drooping when you wear it, and it will show on the front of the apron, so make sure it is neat.

7. Remove the pin from the centre top. Place the ribbon face down on the back of the apron, pin the centre of the ribbon to the centre of the apron, positioning it so that it matches up with the top edge of the apron but extends beyond the edge of the fabric.

8. Sew the ribbon and apron together, making sure you fasten off the ends of the sewing firmly with a couple of back stitches.

9. Turn the apron over and iron the seam flat, with the ribbon up and the fabric downwards (run the tip of the iron between the two). Then fold the ribbon over the top of the apron and iron again, so the ribbon covers the seam. Pin the ribbon in place along the top of the apron, and stitch all the way along the top edge, close to the fold and then down the side to the other ribbon edge. At the other end, sew down the side and then along the other edge of the ribbon. You need to sew in the same direction on both sides of the ribbon or it will pull out of shape.

10. Check the length of the ties and adjust as desired. Finish the ends of the ribbon by turning under a tiny hem and stitching it in place.

Tip

+ A vintage or patterned tea towel would be perfect for the main fabric.

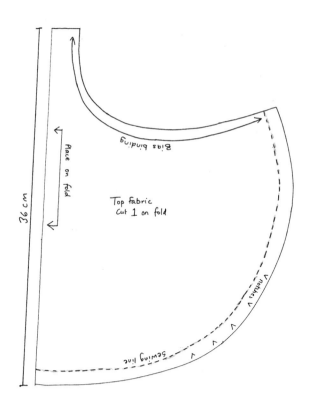

Bias binding

Place on fold

36 cm

Top fabric
Cut 1 on fold

notches

Sewing line

figure 1

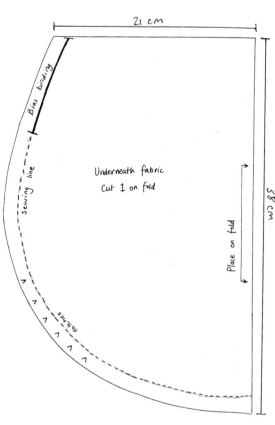

21 cm

Bias binding

Sewing line

Underneath fabric
Cut 1 on fold

Place on fold

38 cm

notches

figure 2

About Ruth

Ruth trained as a museum curator, and specialised in textile and fashion history. After leaving her job with the V&A Museum in London, she set up her own business, making fashion and home accessories such as bags, scarves and cushions. She is influenced by her background in textiles, and uses vintage or recycled materials alongside traditional techniques including pleating, layering, appliqué and quilting. As well as running her business and her website (*www.ruthsinger.com*), Ruth also continues to teach textiles history in museums, schools and arts organisations in Britain.

Jenni Hampshire
WINGS OF DESIRE

These cherub wings are easy to make, eco-friendly and so much cooler than traditional, big angel wings. They are made using long white feathers, which is good for fancy dress, but try more colourful versions for use as a wall-hanging. Pair them with the tiara (see page 59) for the alternative fairy-princess look—or just enjoy wearing them for no good reason at all.

Materials

+ Corrugated card
+ Newspaper
+ Masking tape
+ 2–3 m ribbon
+ All-purpose glue
  (preferably a spray adhesive)
+ Long feathers and about four
  or five little bags of small, soft
  feathers in a variety of colours
+ A small feather boa or marabou
  trim in corresponding colours
+ Other 'fancy' feathers (optional)

Instructions

1. Draw the outline of a pair of cherub wings onto the cardboard. Make the wings stubbier than you think they should be, as the long feathers will add length, and leave a small strip of card connecting the wings. Cut out this shape with scissors.

2. Add bulk to the wings. To do this, scrunch up a dense ball of newspaper, and tape this down at the base of one of the wings. Match this on the other wing. Turn the wings over and repeat this process. Choose one side to be the inside (the side which sits against your back) and one to be the outside (the side which the long feathers will be glued to). On the inside, tape down rolls of newspaper just along the upper edge, and on the outside tape down a triangle of bunched up newspaper to cover the entire remainder of the card. This is the most important stage, as building this shape gives the wings a life-like appearance and slight weight for balance on your back.

3. Cover this entire form with masking tape to provide a better base for gluing the feathers onto. Also, you can use this stage to push and pull the wings about so that they curve away from your back instead of sitting flat like most of the wings you can buy. Both of these are optional.

4. Wrap the ribbons around the middle of the wings, and glue or tie them in place, leaving a good length of ribbon free (this will be the harness, to tie the wings to your back). The end of the ribbons will be obscured by the marabou trim so don't worry about being really neat.

5. Now you are ready to start putting feathers down. Have a think about pattern and colour, and start on the inside of a wing, using small feathers. You can use the marabou trim to fill in a roughly circular shape at the bottom.

6. Repeat this pattern on the other inside wing.

7. Now give them time to dry (about half an hour or more) so that you can work on the outside, without ruining what you've just done.

8. Flip the wings over, and prop up the wing you intend to start on so that the long feathers will not be squashed against the table as you're trying to glue them in place.

9. Sort the feathers from longest to shortest (or thickest to thinnest), and glue these in place along the edge of the wing, with longest or thickest at the top corner—you'll have to use tough glue for this. Then leave them to dry for a while. If you don't have enough feathers, cut some in half and shape the tips to make the small feathers at the bottom of the wing.

10. Choose more colours and glue soft small feathers down in layers on top of the base of the long feathers, just like you did on the inside of the wings. Don't put any marabou trim (or feather boa) down on this side yet.

11. Once fully dry, repeat this process on the outside of the other wing. And then let this dry too.

12. Now you can finish the wings by gluing the last of the marabou trim down. Cover the rest of the wings on the outside, and then wrap it around the middle to cover the ribbons on both sides. Let this dry.

13. Ta da! Now you can try them on. Get someone to help whilst you put the ribbons over your shoulders, under your arms, and back up between the middle of the wings so that you can tie them to themselves at the top. The wings should sit on your shoulder blades and point upwards elegantly towards the sky, like a bird about to take off.

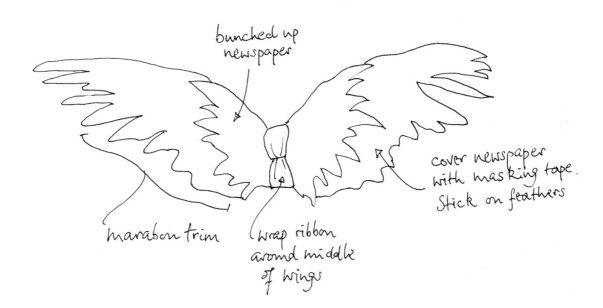

bunched up
newspaper

cover newspaper
with masking tape.
Stick on feathers

marabou trim

wrap ribbon
around middle
of wings

About Jenni

Jenni turned to craft in her final year of university as a rebellion against fine art, which she was studying at the time. She started playing with feathers and papier mâché, building costume wings and heads, and was surprised to find it a really rewarding, creative experience. Jenni is a firm believer in the joys of crafting: "What I think is more important than authorship is to re-interpret things through making. Therefore I would like you to remake my angel/bird wings and enjoy changing the ideas to fit yourself."

Victoria Woodcock

THE 'TIE IT UP' TOP

Sewing stretch jersey can be a bit of a nightmare. The trick is to use a bit of stretchy interfacing and it's plain sailing. This top is great for the summer but also works over a t-shirt or a polo neck. The straps are interchangeable, so, in a matter of moments it can be transformed from a grungy vest with bits of string or old shoelaces as straps, to a glamorous, flouncy top with a wide silk scarf.

Materials

+ Stretch jersey fabric (or a big old t-shirt)—the amount depends on the size you are making
+ Matching coloured thread
+ .5 m stretchy iron-on (fusible) interfacing
+ Tailors' chalk
+ Sewing machine
+ An old silk scarf/t-shirt/shirt/ string and beads/shoelaces

Instructions

1. Measure up before you buy fabric, so you don't end up buying too much. To find the width of fabric you need, measure your widest part. It's probably your chest, but it might be your belly or your hips (if you want a long top). Add 5 to this number (this will ensure that your creation isn't skin-tight) and divide by 2. For example, if your chest size is 91 cm, add 5 to this number, so 96 cm. Then divide by 2, to get 48.

2. You probably want your top to be around 46–51 cm long —this will make a nice long top down to your hips. If you want it a bit shorter or longer, measure from where you want the neckline to rest—a couple of inches below your clavicle, down to wear you would like the fabric to sit on your stomach or hips. If you want to hem the bottom, make it a few centimetres longer, but as jersey fabric doesn't fray, this is not essential.

3. Stick some pieces of paper together and draw a rectangle using these measurements.

4. Now measure from the neckline point to underneath your arms. Measure straight down the centre of your body and imagine a line running from beneath your armpit round to the measuring tape. This should be around about 8 cm—don't make this measurement much less than 8 cm as the last thing you want is it to be too tight around your pits.

5. If your bust is wider than your belly, then measure from the neckline point to where your stomach curves in. Mark these points on your rectangle and draw lines across the width.

6. Now measure across where the neckline will sit. The trick is to wear a bra and measure either side of the straps. On the middle of the top edge of the rectangle, mark a line this length. Now connect the end points of this line to the line below (let's call it the armpit line) with a curve, joining the armpit line at least 3 cm away from the edge of the rectangle. Extend the rectangle with a box the width of the neckline and 7.5 cm high (this is to make a tube for the straps).

7. If you want to curve it in slightly at the waist, place your pencil on the belly line about 3 cm in from the edge and draw a line that curves up and gradually merges with the edge of the rectangle. Repeat downwards.

8. Cut out your pattern and place it on the wrong side of your fabric, at least 2 cm from the edge. Ensure that the stretch runs horizontally. Pin the pattern and draw around it with tailors' chalk. Reposition at least 5 cm away from the first trace and repeat.

9. Now cut strips of interfacing, so that the stretch will run the same way as the fabric, and iron them over the chalk lines at the side of the body. Don't worry about making them particularly neat, nobody is going to see them. If you can no longer see the chalk line clearly, retrace it with a biro on top of the interfacing. Stick another 5 cm wide strip below the top line of the tube flap and below the neckline. Use the pattern to trace the curve from the neckline onto the interfacing and turn it into a 2 cm shape. Make two from each side and iron them neatly underneath the armpit curve, touching the chalk line.

10. Now cut out the shapes 2 cm around the chalked lines. Place the pieces on top of one another—right sides facing. Match up the lines and pin together. Sew the two pieces together along the sidelines. If your machine has a stretch stitch function use this, if not opt for a straight running stitch of length 2.5.

11. You don't have to hem the armpit curves, just cut neatly along the line up to the top of the flap. But if you want to hem them here's what you do:

12. Cut 'V' shapes from the 2 cm selvedge around the curve— cut close to the line (about 3 mm away) but do not touch it.

13. Iron over the triangles and the selvedge from the flap (you only need to cut the V shapes on a curve not a straight edge).

14. Set the sewing machine to a straight running stitch of 2.5 and on the wrong side of the fabric (so you can see what you're doing) sew a line 2 mm from the edge. Be sure to sew through the continuous strip of material before the V-shaped nicks.

15. Cut off the triangle shapes close to the sewn line.

16. Now to make the tube: fold over about 3 cm of the flap and iron. Fold again at the neckline—the beginning of the next strip of interfacing—and iron. Pin into place and sew a line across the width of the top through all layers. Repeat on the other side.

17. The straps can be made from any long strip threaded through the front tube, passed over one shoulder through the back tube and tied at the other shoulder. You need a strip around 2 m long to be able to fasten it in a generous bow.

How to make the tie from an old blouse

18. Cut the sleeves off, snip down the seams and cut the cuff off to make two flat sections.

19. Cut one or two sections of a similar width from the back and one from either side of the buttons on the front. Join these five segments together into a long strip by placing two pieces together—right sides facing—and sewing a line 2 cm away from the shorter edges.

20. Continue by placing another segment on top of one of the two joined together and repeat. When they are all sewn together, fold the strip in half—right sides facing—and iron. Make a tube by sewing a straight line an equal distance away from the fold and never less than 2 cm away from the rough edges.

21. Turn the tube inside out, turn in the rough edges at either end and sew to close. Thread it through the two tubes on the top, sling it on and fasten with flair.

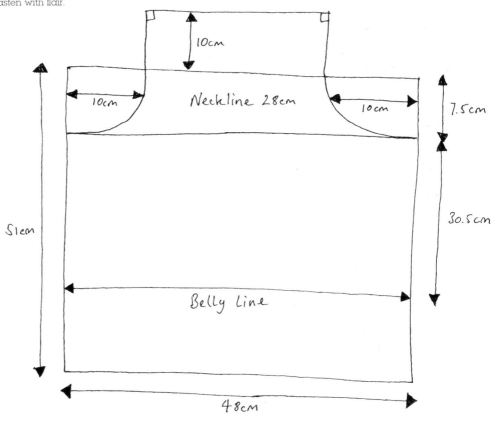

UNICORN BELIEVER

What is the point of slaving over a sampler when no one gets to see your handiwork? Let people know you believe in unicorns by stitching one onto a dreamy satin jacket! Or anywhere and everywhere else for that matter.

Materials

+ Embroidery floss
  (pick your favourite colors)
+ Embroidery hoop (optional)
+ Embroidery needle (this one
  used a size 3 crewel needle)
+ Carbon transfer paper (sometimes
  called dressmaker's carbon)
+ Photocopy of pattern from
  the book
+ A lightweight windbreaker

Instructions

1. Take this book to work and make a copy of the unicorn pattern, enlarging it to the required size.

2. Trace the image onto your jacket using a sheet of carbon transfer paper. This usually comes in black, red, blue or white. Choose a colour you'll be able to see against the fabric. Place the sheet face down between the image and the cloth and draw over the design with a biro.

3. If you have opted to use an embroidery hoop, separate the two sections and lay the imprinted cloth across the non-adjustable hoop so that the pattern is within the hoop (or part of it, if the design is bigger than the hoop). Now place the adjustable hoop over these and press down. Make sure the top hoop is not too tight, or you will stress the fabric. Before tightening, gently pull your fabric taut like a drum. Once your fabric is pulled evenly across the hoop, tighten the screw.

4. Pick the line you want to embroider first and cut a length of floss or thread about 30–35 cm long (the length of your thumb and forefinger to your elbow) in an appropriate colour. Thread the needle, and make a knot at the opposite end. Pick a point at the start of a line and bring your needle up from under the fabric until you hit the knot. Now, bring the needle back down through, and you've made a stitch!

5. You follow the pattern with a continuous line by using a split stitch: make a small stitch, and bring the needle up for the next stitch through the centre of the previous stitch, 'splitting' the threads (see page 26).

6. Keep stitching until your unicorn comes to life!

Tips

+ Before you take needle and thread to a beloved jacket, practice on a scrap piece of cotton fabric or a plain tea towel.

+ For details, such as the eye, split the floss, so that you're only using three of the six strands. This will create finer lines.

About Jenny

Jenny Hart is an internationally published artist/illustrator living and working in Austin, Texas. She founded Sublime Stitching (www.sublimestitching.com) in 2001 to take embroidery where it had never been before with hip and stylish embroidery patterns and the first all-in-one embroidery starter kits. A noted pioneer of the contemporary DIY movement, Jenny's work has featured in many zines and publications, including *Teen Vogue*, *Bust*, *JANE*, *ReadyMade*, *Nylon* and *The Wall Street Journal*, as well as on a number of television programmes.
www.jennyhart.net

Lovelylovely
RA RA APRON

This sexy number is a little bit girly, a little bit handy and a little bit naughty. You can make it out of fabric, plastic, or as the Lovely girls do—out of PVC.

Materials

+ 1 m fabric
+ 4 m of scraps of contrasting fabric for bindings
+ Matching thread
+ Pinking shears (or sharp scissors)

Instructions

1. Cut out the fabric pieces diagonally as shown in fig. 1. Add seam allowances of 1 cm.

2. Cut out your fabric for the apron skirt (fig. 2).

3. Hem the side seams of the skirt.

4. Make the bias bindings. You will need at least 4 m. Cut diagonal strips of fabric 3 cm wide. Fold over and iron the edges (fig. 3).

5. Cut out crescent shapes for the frills. These need to be longer than the width of the skirt, so that they rouche up properly.

6. Sew binding onto the frills. Pin a few tucks so that the length of the fabric fits the width of the apron (fig. 4).

7. Assemble: Sew the frills onto the apron skirt as shown in fig. 5. For the apron strings, sew a length of bias binding to the waist.

About Lovelylovely

Lovelylovely is the result of a collaboration between Louise Scott-Smith, fashion designer, and graphic designer Georgia Vaux. Their love of handicrafts comes from their interest in the irregularities and detail of something handmade. They like playing with different materials—purposefully mismatching them to the item they are producing. This contradictory aesthetic is at the heart of all their products. Check out their website on www.lovelylovely.net.

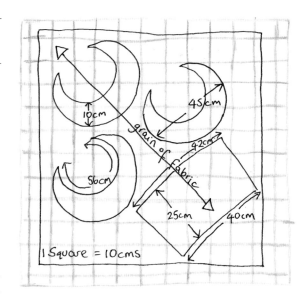

figure 1

figure 2

figure 3

figure 4

figure 5

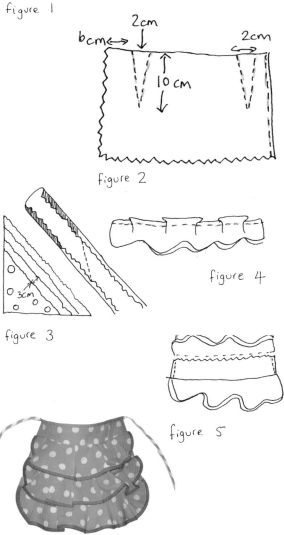

Victoria Woodcock
SKINNY RIBBING SCARF

Once you've got to grips with knit and purl stitches, do what every other new knitter in the history of time has done—make a scarf. A ribbed scarf will hold its shape well and can be worn by boys and girls alike. There is apparently a curse surrounding knitting a jumper for your loved one—all the hard work will only end in tears and a break up, so it goes. But this does not apply to scarves, so knit one for your sweetheart to keep them hot under the collar!

Materials
+ 2–4 balls of worsted weight yarn (depending on how long you want the scarf to be)
+ Knitting needles to match the thickness of the yarn
+ Yarn needle

Instructions:

1. Cast on about 30–40 stitches. Or for a long skinny number, cast on just 20 or so—it doesn't matter how many stitches you have so long as it is an even number.

2. Work a k1, p1 rib the length of the scarf. Remember, after you have knit one stitch, you need to bring the yarn to the front of the needles to make a purl. To return to a knit stitch you take the yarn back between the needles so that it is at the back again. Here is what you do:

   All rows: *k1, p1; repeat from * across

   This basically means k1, p1, k1, p1, k1, p1 and on and on, until you have no more stitches. Turn round and do the same. The rib works by making a 'V' row (knit on one side, purl on the other) next to a bump row (purl on one side, knit on the other).

3. Keep on ribbing until you have a rectangle long enough to wrap and tie around your neck. Keep track of your stitches by counting them at regular intervals.

4. Cast off!

Tip

+ Some knitters like to slip the first stitch and knit the last stitch of every row to make a neat edge. To give this a go, just do this instead: All rows: sl1, *k1, p1; repeat from * to last stitch, k1.

Victoria Woodcock
BOW DOWN BELT

You may have seen a certain bow belt with a hefty price tag doing the rounds in the fashion magazines. A bow at your waist is a design classic and the best thing about making one yourself is that you can fit it snug to your gut—it's a cinch!

Materials

+ About 50 cm of fabric in a width big enough to fit around your waist
+ Lining material (the same amount)
+ 3–4 corsetry hooks and eyes

Instructions

1. Measure your waist, and don't breathe in! Be honest with yourself, you want a snug fit but you don't want to bulge out either side of the belt. Add 4 cm to your measurement—this will allow for the overlap of fastening.

2. Use this measurement to draw a rectangle on paper with half this number as the length and 8–12 cm as the width (depending on how wide you want your belt to be).

3. Fold the width of your fabric in half so that the wrong side is facing you, the rectangle should fit comfortably across the folded width. Draw around it, and cut through both layers of fabric 1–2 cm around the lines. Place to one side for the time being—it will be used to make the bow.

4. Now return to the paper rectangle. If you make a belt that is completely rectangular, it isn't going to be very comfortable —it should get thinner at either end so as to fit in the curve of your back. Mark the mid point of the rectangle and then at one end, mark off a section no wider than 6 cm in the middle of the line. Now draw straight diagonal lines up from these points to the edge, just before the mid point and cut out (fig. 1).

5. Again, place this shape on the fold of the fabric, draw and cut (not forgetting 1–2 cm selvedge). On both thicknesses of fabric mark the midpoint. Cut and mark the lining fabric in the same way.

6. Now ask yourself the somewhat intimate question, "Am I an innie or an outie?" If your stomach curves inwards you will want to add some dart shaping, if your belly protrudes out further than your hips and ribs you might not need to bother. Wrap the belt shape around you waist. If there is excess fabric in the middle of the fabric at your sides then proceed with some darts.

7. You probably want to make a dart about 1 cm deep. To do so, fold the main fabric of the belt at the two midpoints so that the right sides of the fabric are facing, and iron. In the middle of the fold draw a point 1 cm in from the edge and from this point draw curved lines that run into the fold before the pattern lines on either side (fig. 2). Sew along this line from the middle to the fold, run a few stitches along the fold as close to the edge as possible. If using a machine, do not backstitch to secure, instead cut the threads and tie them together. This will prevent the dart from puckering. Sew from the middle in the other direction.

8. Repeat for the mid point on the other side and wrap the belt around your waist again. If there is still an amount of excess fabric, make the dart a bit deeper, say 1.5 cm.

9. Make the same sized darts in the same manner on the lining fabric.

10. Line up the two belt pieces, right sides together, and pin along the chalk lines. Sew along the two long lines and one of the ends. Turn the belt the right way around and iron so that the fabric and lining are directly on top of one another. Tuck in the rough edges at the un-sewn end, pin and iron.

11. Sew all the way around the belt on the right side, 4 mm in from the edge and hand-sew hooks and eyes at either end. Sew hooks onto the right side at one end, about 1.5 cm in, with the hook part facing towards the end. Sew the eyes on to the wrong side of the other end about 2 cm in (or where needed for a snug fit) with the eye part facing the end. Make sure they are equally spaced and line up.

12. For the bow, return to the initial rectangle. With the fabric folded in half (as it was cut) sew along the two long lines. Turn it the right way around and iron. Feed one end into the other to form a circle, and sew into place. Press the circle flat with the seam in the middle.

13. Fold over a section of the remaining fabric (right sides facing) and draw a rectangle 15 × 4 cm to form the centre of the bow. Cut out 1 cm around the lines, sew the two layers together along the two 15 cm lines and turn the right way around.

14. Position this tube in the middle of the flattened circle of fabric. Pull the tube around the fabric to form the bow shape (fig. 3). Cover the join at the back with the tube and hand sew into place. Use a few neat overhand stitches at the centre and the four corners to attach the bow to the middle of the belt. Bow down to me!

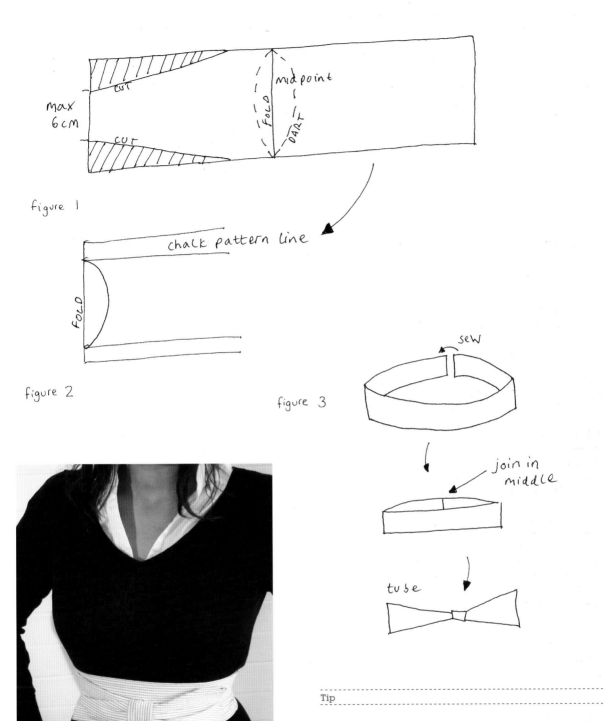

figure 1

max
6cm

CUT

CUT

FOLD

midpoint

DART

chalk pattern line

FOLD

figure 2

figure 3

sew

join in
middle

tube

Tip

+ If your fabric isn't wide enough to fit the whole belt on, make
it up in parts. For the bow (step 3) draw around the rectangle
twice on unfolded fabric. For the belt, cut the paper pattern at
the midpoint (after step 4) and place the rectangle part on the
fold of the fabric to make the front section. Then draw around
the back sloping section twice on unfolded fabric. Join up the
three parts. This way the joins will be at the sides where you
position the darts. Using this technique you would be able to
use an old shirt for the main fabric.

ECO SHOPPER

Ditch the plastic bags for good with this stylish crocheted shopper. Make it doubly good for the environment by recycling an old bed sheet.

Materials

+ 1 bed sheet—any size will do
+ 6.5 mm or 7 mm crochet hook
+ 4 locking or split ring stitch markers
+ Sewing thread to match bed sheet
+ Metal measuring tape (available at hardware stores)
+ Fabric dye (optional)

Instructions

1. To make the yarn, wash, dry and iron your sheet. Spread it out on floor and with the metal measuring tape and tailors' chalk, measure and draw lines approximately 2 cm apart. Do not extend the lines along the whole length of the fabric, but stop 2 cm before the edge, and start the lines at alternate ends (fig. 1).

2. You will be cutting along these lines to create a series of zigzagging strips. To form a continuous strip, cut almost all the way to the end (where your lines end 2 cm before the edge) and then turn and cut down the next line from the edge to 2 cm before the opposite edge. If you accidentally cut an end, just sew the two strips together with needle and thread. Wind the strip into a ball as you cut, otherwise the 'yarn' will get tangled.

3. If you want to dye your sheet you need to wind it into a skein. To do this wind it around the back of a chair and tie the ends together to secure. Remove the loop from the chair and grab hold of the two ends with either hand. Twist as much as you can and then bring your hands together and the twists should keep it folded over. Dye it with fabric dye following the instructions on the package—polycotton blends will not achieve a saturated colour. Be sure to wash after dyeing to get all the residual dye out. Place the skein back on to the back of a chair or over your knees and wind into a ball again.

4. Get your hook, and crochet away. See page 28 for help.

Pattern Stitches
ch = chain
r = round or row
sc = single crochet
sl = slip stitch

+ Round 1: ch5, sl stitch into the 1st stitch at base of chain to join in the round.
+ Round 2: ch1, place marker in this stitch, work 7sc into the loop (8sc).
+ Round 3: *ch2, 1sc into the next sc; repeat from * 7 times more (8 loops—looks like a flower with 8 petals).
+ Round 4: *ch2, 1sc into the next loop, ch2, 1 sc into the same loop, ch2, 1 sc into the next loop; repeat from * 3 times more (12 loops).
+ Round 5: *ch2, 1sc into the next loop; rep from * 11 times more.
+ Round 6: *ch3, 1sc into the next loop; repeat from * 11 times more.
+ Round 7: *(ch3, 1 sc into the next loop, ch3, 1 sc into the same loop, ch3, 1 sc into the next Loop); repeat from * to end (18 loops).
+ Round 8: *ch3, 1sc into the next loop; repeat from * 17 times more.
+ Round 9: *ch3, 1 sc into the next loop, ch3, 1 sc into the same loop, ch3, 1 sc into the next loop; repeat from * to end (28 loops).
+ Round 10: *ch3, 1sc into the next loop; repeat from * 27 times more.
+ Round 11–Round 19: Repeat Round 10.
+ Round 20: *ch2, 1sc into the next loop; repeat from *to end.
+ Round 21: *ch1, 1sc into the next loop; repeat from * to end.
+ Round 22: *1sc in each sc, 1sc in each loop; repeat from * to end.

5. To make the handles divide the rim of bag into four equal sections (you can eyeball it) and place marker at each of the three remaining quarters (you should already have one marker in place that was marking your rounds).

6. For the first handle ch30 loosely, make sure the chain is not twisted and attach it with a sl stitch to the rim of the bag at the next marker to the left. Turn and work back along the chain, 1sc in each chain stitch to end, 1sc in rim of bag. Turn, and work back along the chain again, 1sc in each sc to end, 1sc in rim of bag. Cut yarn and fasten off, remove markers from this handle.

7. For the second handle make a sl stitch at the marker left of the handle you just finished. Repeat instructions for the first handle. Sew in the ends with a needle and a matching colour of thread.

Tips

+ In the first 4 rounds count the number of stitches/loops at the end of each round to be sure it is correct. If you make too many your bag will be too wide later.

+ To keep track of your rows place a marker on the first stitch of the round after it has been completed.

+ The bag will stretch with the weight you carry, so work tighter rather than loose.

+ To join a second ball of yarn sew the ends together with needle and matching thread. Also, instead of weaving ends in, sew them down.

+ For beginner crochet help, see the following resources: about.com, http://crochet.about.com or crochet me, http://crochetme.com

+ If you want to use yarn you will need approximately 140 m of ribbon yarn, 1 cm to 1.5 cm wide.

About Hayley

In her last incarnation Hayley was an Art & Architectural Historian at the University of Toronto. Now she's a purveyor of string and an artist. She owns the knitting store Knit-O-Matic in Toronto, Canada, where she lives with her lovebird Pluto. You can find them both at *www.knitomatic.com*.

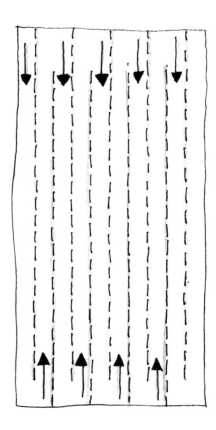

ALL THAT GLITTERS

JEWELLERY TO COMPLEMENT THE LOOK

+ Happy Hemper
+ Button Up Badge Necklace
+ Brazen Barbie Bling
+ Papier Mâché Jewellery
+ Knitted Floral Fancy
+ Ballsy Necklace
+ Blow Your Own Trumpet Tiara
+ Beady-Eyed Lizard
+ Vinyl Cuff
+ Papercut Necklace

Sophie Parker
HAPPY HEMPER

Hemp is swiftly becoming the yarn of choice for discerning, ecologically minded fashionistas. It is also an ideal material to make jewellery—it looks rustic but can be given a modern twist with plastic beads, it goes soft with wear, it's good to work with and it's biodegradable! It's also very cheap, so you might as well buy a ball, or two. Macramé is a lot easier than it looks—once you knot you can't stop!

Materials

+ A ball of hemp yarn— or at the very least, a 3 m length of hemp. Fairly thin, polished hemp works best for jewellery making
+ Beads with holes large enough to comfortably slide down the hemp
+ A clipboard (or a foot)

Instructions

1. Cut two lengths of hemp. Each length should be six times the circumference of your neck. It's easiest to wrap the hemp around your neck three times, double that length over, and cut.

2. Fold each length of hemp in two, so that there are four strands of equal length to work with. Fix it to your clipboard or, as depicted, around your toe, to keep it taut and secure (fig.1).

3. Separate the strands and lay the outer two to one side for a moment. The inside two will be your 'knot bearers' and won't move until you come to slide the beads on. Fix your knot bearers down, or if you're using your feet, wrap them around your leg. Make sure they are taut (fig. 2).

4. Take the right hand outer strand. Cross it over the front (not underneath) of the knot bearers to the left. Then push it underneath the left strand (fig. 3).

5. Then you've got to do the same inverted. This sounds complicated, but you're only making a basic knot. Feed the left over to the right side, but this time underneath the knot bearers. The original right strand has formed a loop—feed the left strand up through it.

6. Pull it taut. This is the first part of the square knot.

7. To complete the square knot, repeat steps 4–6 again, but this time starting with the strand that is now on the left. Make sure the knots are always taut; otherwise you will get loops, which look a bit scruffy (fig. 4).

8. Continue knotting on alternative sides for as long as looks suitable. When you feel ready for a bead, free the knot bearing strands and pass a bead onto them. If the bead is not big enough to slide over both, then thread it onto one strand only (fig. 5). Push it up to the knots, and complete at least one square knot around it to secure, before putting on another bead. (You might want more hemp between each bead, and if so, just make more square knots before the next bead).

9. Continue for as long as you want, measuring against your neck (or wrist, or ankle, etc.).

10. There are two ways to finish off your piece. One is to tie a knot, leaving a length of four strands free so that the wearer can tie the choker tight with the loose strands to his/her requirements. Or you could square knot until practically the end of the length of your hemp and position a final bead to act as a clasp by feeding it though the initial loop.

11. And that's it—you're finished! But that's just the beginning! You can experiment with different patterns, (for example, if instead of alternating the side you knot from, you always start the knot from the right-hand-side, you get a lovely twisted effect that looks like strands of DNA), different types of hemp and different beads.

Tips

+ If you ever forget which side you should be knotting from, count 'right left right left', etc., on each visible line from the top of the knot bearing strands.

+ You can use clear nail varnish to seal the final knots, if you're afraid they might come undone. It really works and no-one would know!

About Sophie

A recent English graduate, Sophie's time is mostly filled groaning over application forms and CV templates, and worrying about how her overdraft will eventually be paid off. In between, she spends her time making hemp jewellery, which she has been doing for five years now, ever since she discovered a particularly detailed macramé website. Check her work out on: www.barmymacrame.otf.org.uk.

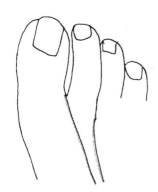

figure 1

figure 2

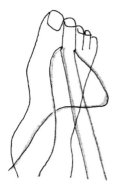

figure 3

figure 4

figure 5

Victoria Woodcock

BUTTON UP
BADGE NECKLACE

I know—it's a badge, but across the Atlantic they call it a button. You can pick up badges for free all over the place, but if you prefer a classy brooch on your lapel what do you do with all those old badges? With a few tools you can fashion up an eye-catching piece of badge jewellery.

Materials

+ Badges (probably around 20 depending on the size of the badges and your collar size)
+ Hammer
+ Small flat-head nail
+ Block of wood or a chunky magazine
+ Jewellery making round nosed pliers
+ A short length of metal chain
+ Metal clasp
+ Wire cutters
+ A few jump rings

Instructions

1. Collect some badges. The best ones to use are the ones with a metal back and a pin sprung into place with a metal half circle. You can also use the ones made with a plastic back and a safety pin set into the plastic. Homemade ones with the plastic circle holding the pin aren't going to work.

2. Arrange your badges, by twizzling the backs so that the clasps are all on the same side. Using a pair of pliers, pull the pin out to the side of the badge and snip off the sharp pinpoint with a pair of wire-cutters—you don't want this sticking into your neck.

3. Position the badge, facing up, on a block of wood or a chunky magazine, and using the hammer, knock the nail through the badge about 3–4 mm away from its edge, on the opposite side to where the pin sticks out. Remove the nail, leaving a small, clean hole. Repeat for each badge.

4. Push the pin on one badge through the hole on the front of another and then twist the pin around the edge of the badge to secure. Hold the pin with the pliers and turn it under the badge and then clasp the edge of the badge and the pin underneath, squeezing together to tighten up the join. This should result in the badges overlapping slightly with one another.

5. The last badge in the chain needs a hole on both sides to attach the clasp. Place a couple of jump rings (these are the connecting hoops used in jewellery-making) through the holes on either end: use the pliers to pull the hoop apart, attach it to the badge, slip on a length of chain and close the hoop. Attach a clasp with jump rings at the ends of the chain, and button up!

Jasmin Hollingum
BRAZEN BARBIE BLING

The great thing about Barbie is that she's nothing if not controversial—whether you're appalled by what she stands for, or aspire to her peculiar proportions, these accessories are sure to get you noticed.

Materials

+ 1 pair of plastic Barbie shoes
+ 1 plastic Barbie hat
+ 1 pair silver ear hooks
+ 6 mm split rings (split rings are like tiny key rings)
+ 4 mm split rings
+ 1 key ring
+ Small pliers (try using tweezers if you don't have any)
+ Pin or sewing needle
+ Tea light and matches

Tip

+ If you are making the earrings for yourself, recycle ear hooks and split rings from earrings you no longer wear. If you are making earrings for a friend, buy new sterling silver ear hooks. They make a cheap and fun gift.

Instructions

Barbie shoe earrings:

1. First you will need to make a hole in the top of each shoe. Light the tea light and hold the tip of the pin or needle in the flame for a few seconds. Insert the pin into the back of the shoe, close to the top. The pin will go straight through as the heat melts the plastic. Make the hole a bit bigger by moving the pin in a circular motion.

2. Take a 6 mm split ring and thread it through the hole in the top of the shoe. You may need to use the pliers to help you open up the ring and squeeze it shut.

3. To create the chain, attach 4 mm split rings one on top of the other with the 6 mm ring as the base. Thread the top ring through the loop at the bottom of the ear hook. Using the pliers, twist the loop so that the front of the shoe is pointing away from the ear hook.

Barbie hat key ring:

1. Make a hole near the edge of the brim of the hat, as you did in step 1 of the Barbie shoe earrings.

2. Thread a 6 mm split ring through the hole in the hat.

3. With this ring as the base, make a chain with the 4 mm split rings until it is the desired length.

4. Thread the top ring of the chain onto the key ring. Slip on your keys and jump into your pink Caddy!

About Jasmin

Jasmin was inspired to craft at an early age by her mum's copy of *Wild Knitting*. Many childhood hours were spent furiously knotting friendship bracelets and making rag rugs. The discovery of craftster.org sealed her fate, and over the years she has delved into the joys of knitting, crochet and embroidery. When she's not crafting, her time is spent playing violin and French horn, singing in her band, Shady Bard *www.shadybard.co.uk* and running her Etsy shop *http://jasminalice.etsy.com*.

PAPIER MÂCHÉ JEWELLERY

Paper is such a versatile material. Mashing up paper bits in water (it may have a fancy French name but that is pretty much what papier mâché is!) is fun at any age. By adding some glittery bits into the mix the result is a bit more glitzy—and great for making jewellery.

This project is very straightforward—but be warned, the papier mâché takes a good two days to dry, so don't expect instant gratification!

Materials

+ Scrap paper, card and other items, such as silver and gold foil
+ Liquidiser or blender and bowl
+ Matt or gloss varnish
+ Sponge
+ Rolling pin (optional)
+ Round-ended scissors (either nail scissors or specialist craft scissors)
+ Paintbrush
+ Paper clips—standard size for the necklace, small for the bracelet (these need to be flat paperclips, not the ones with the protruding lip)
+ Masking tape
+ 20 × 2 cm and 1 × 2.5 cm metal washers for the necklace
+ 10 × 1.5 cm and 1 × 2 cm metal washers for the bracelet
+ All-purpose glue

Instructions

1. Begin by making the papier mâché: tear up scrap paper, card and other items you wish to include, into postage stamp size pieces and mix together thoroughly.

2. Fill the liquidiser/blender half full with lukewarm water. Add the scrap materials and leave for a couple of minutes to allow them to soak. DO NOT overfill or you will put too much of a strain on the mechanism and it will overheat.

3. Blend on a low to medium speed for five to ten seconds, and then blend on high for another 20 to 25 seconds to create a pulp mixture. Continue to blend until you are satisfied with the consistency of the pulp—it depends on whether you want a textured surface or a smooth one.

4. Place two newspapers side by side on your kitchen table, then place two layers of kitchen roll on top of each of the newspapers. Pour the pulp out on top of one of the prepared surfaces and spread the mixture out with your hands until there is an even thickness. You may find it useful to use a rolling pin. Don't make it too thick or it will be difficult to cut later on.

5. Press a dry sponge on the pulp to remove excess water. Ring out the sponge regularly. Continue to do this until the pulp is virtually dry.

6. Flip the papier mâché on to the other dry newspaper surface to work on the underside, sponging off the excess water. If the pulp is really soggy, you may have to repeat these steps with fresh newspaper and kitchen roll.

7. When you are satisfied that enough liquid has been removed, and the mixture holds together well, place the papier mâché in a warm environment and leave to dry. This may take two or three days, depending on the ambient temperature.

8. Whilst the papier mâché is drying, make the jewellery fittings. The procedure is the same for both the bracelet and the necklace. Link the paper clips so that they are running in the same direction. If you are making the necklace, make sure the paperclip chain fits snugly around your throat. Too long, and it will not sit properly.

9. Stretch out the paperclips in a straight line. Gently lift the smaller inner loop of the clip and slide a washer (wrong-side up) in between the two parts of the clip. Ensure that the washer is positioned centrally, with the end loops of the paperclip clearly visible on either side. Continue until all the washers of the same size have been placed (fig. 1). Glue the paperclips to the washers and leave to dry overnight.

10. When the papier mâché is dry, decide which side you prefer, and apply a coat of varnish to this surface. This binds the papier mâché even further and makes it easier to cut.

11. On the papier mâché, draw around the spare 2 cm washer (for the bracelet) and 2.5 cm washer (for the necklace), matching the number of discs to the number of washers for each item of jewellery.

12. Cut out the discs very carefully with the rounded scissors. The discs need to be a little bit bigger than the washers so that the paper clip links are concealed. It may be necessary to trim the discs slightly to ensure that they sit properly on the mountings.

13. Once you have the correct number of discs, line them up, wrong side up (this is the side which hasn't been varnished). Take one disc at a time, put a liberal amount of glue on the disc and carefully place the first washer fixing on top of the disc. Hold firmly together. Make sure the washer is in the centre of the disc and that the right (rounded) side of the washer is uppermost. In other words, the wrong side of the disc and the wrong side of the washer are being glued together. Continue until all discs and washers have been glued together. You may find it useful to secure the piece with masking tape and remove when the glue has dried.

14. When the glue is dry, apply varnish to the underside and sides of the papier mâché discs. When this is dry, you may wish to apply a second coat of varnish to ensure the item is watertight—it would be a shame for the jewellery to disintegrate at the first spot of rain!

15. Secure a paperclip to both ends of the necklace to fasten. For the bracelet fastening, use the end of the paperclip at one end and hook through the loop of the paperclip at the other end. Make sure you then press the paperclip end flat so that it doesn't stick you in the wrist!

About Amanda

Amanda became interested in crafts thanks to her step-daughter Rosie, who shares her passion for all things artistic. In recent years, Amanda has been involved in silversmithing, glass and silk painting, papier mâché and card making, and runs workshops for adults with learning difficulties at a local drop-in centre. Craft is a welcome antidote to Amanda's professional work activity as a freelance writer and editor. www.editorial.copsewood.net

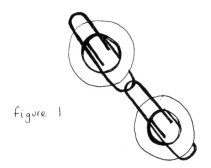

figure 1

Fiona Blakeman
KNITTED FLORAL FANCY

Be sure to wear a flower in your hair... even if you're not going to San Francisco! Get into a hippy clique with a knitted flower clip or brooch.

Materials
+ 1 skein chunky yarn
+ 7 mm knitting needles, or appropriate size for the yarn
+ Yarn needle
+ 1 medium to large button
+ Coordinating thread
+ Kirby grip (for clip)
+ Safety pin (for brooch)

Instructions

1. Don't worry too much about the gauge. The chunkier your wool, the bigger the flower will be. It is quick to make a petal, so just dive straight in:
   + co 3 sts
   + Row 1: k
   + Row 2: p
   + Row 3: sl1, m1, k1, m1, k1 (5 sts)
   + Row 4: P
   + Row 5: sl1, m1, k3, m1, k1 (7 sts)
   + Row 6: p
   + Row 7: k2tog, k3, k2tog (5sts)
   + Row 8: p
   + Row 9: k2tog, k1, k2tog (3sts)
   + Row 10: p1, p2tog (2 sts)

2. Cut the yarn leaving a 15 cm tail. Push the petal to the end of the needle.

3. Knit another 5 petals in the same manner, repeating steps 1 and 2. When you get to the end of the sixth petal, don't cut the yarn.

4. Now knit across all 12 stitches as so: k1, k2tog × 5, k1 (7 sts).

5. Cut the yarn with a 20 cm tail and using the needle thread the yarn through the 7 stitches and slip them off the needle. Pull the yarn tight, forcing the petals to form a flower and tie off in a secure knot. To firm up the centre of the flower, use the excess wool to do a couple of rows of running stitches, joining the petals at the base.

6. The knitted side will make the top of the flower. Weave in all the loose ends and tie off wool at the back of the flower (purl side). The petals do tend to curl up at the edges, so you may want to iron them before attaching the centre.

7. Sew the button firmly into the centre.

For a hair clip
8. After sewing the button to the centre don't cut the thread, hold a hairgrip underneath the flower and pass the sewing needle around the grip and back up through the button. Continue until secure.

For a brooch
9. Pass a safety pin (large enough to fix the flower to a garment firmly but not too large that it can be seen) through the centre of the flower and attach to your desired garment.

Tip

+ If you don't really want a hair clip or a brooch, sew your flower on as a permanent addition to a jumper or a hat. Sew it through the holes on the button directly on the fabric of your choice.

About Fiona

Art student Fiona likes being crafty—especially with her knitting needles and sewing machine. She enjoys nothing more than personalising her clothes with her own handmade accessories.

Victoria Woodcock
BALLSY NECKLACE

Once you begin to break down the cost of costume jewellery a trip to Accessorize will never be quite the same. Don't think that only those with a delicate touch can bejewel, forget beads and tricky wire twists and rip off these chunky, ballsy fabric necklaces.

Materials

+ Scrap of fabric (you need a strip 12 cm × 2 m so a piece 50 × 50 cm would be perfect)
+ 14–20 wooden balls/beads/power balls of roughly 2.5 cm in diameter
+ Needle and thread
+ Clasp (optional)
+ Super glue (optional)

Instructions

1. Steal your roommate's silk scarf and cut it into strips about 12 cm wide (you could also get your fabric from one of your dad's dodgy silk shirts or the curtains at a stranger's house party, or even buy some! But thin, patterned silky fabrics work best).

2. Join enough strips together to form a 2 m long piece: place the right sides together and sew a straight line 2 cm in from the 12 cm edge. Repeat as required.

3. Fold the strip in half lengthways with the fabric joins on the inside and iron. Whilst ironing, turn under about 1 cm or so on all sides (so that no rough edges can be seen).

4. When tying the balls up in the fabric, the trick is to keep the rough ends folded inwards for a neat result. Work from the centre outwards. Tie a knot halfway along the strip. Put a ball in the middle of the fabric and push it tight up against the knot. Wrap the ball up in the material, concealing the edges, and tie a knot on the other side to hold it in place.

5. Continue with more balls either side until you have a string long enough to tie around your neck.

6. At either end, sew the two the sides of the remaining fabric together to keep the edges concealed.

7. You can fasten by sewing or knotting the two ends together; the string needs to be long enough to fit over your head to do this. Alternatively, if you can find a clasp like the one in the photograph, you just twist the end of your fabric, squirt some super glue into the hollow cylinder, and push in the twisted fabric.

Sara Evans
BLOW YOUR OWN
TRUMPET TIARA

Shiny beads and a couple of plastic toys are the perfect materials for a tiara fit for a queen. This one was made with elephants, but you can use anything from dollhouse furniture to Lego men. Perfect for weddings, christmas parties and everyday wear!

Materials
+ Tiara band
+ Wire cutters
+ Flat nose pliers
+ 0.5 mm wire
+ 1 mm wire
+ Beads and jewels of your choice
  (All of the above can be bought
  at craft suppliers)
+ Plastic animals or other small
  objects (available from toyshops)
+ Araldite resin

Instructions

1. Cut approximately 10 cm of the 1 mm wire and use it to attach plastic toys of your choice to the tiara band: cut one end of the wire into a sharp point and insert into the underside of the plastic object. You may need to use the flat nose pliers to grip the wire in order to push it in.

2. Wind the other end of the wire around the tiara band where you want the elephant/other toy to sit. You will need to wind it around at least twice. If it seems a bit wobbly, squeeze it tight with the flat nose pliers. Snip off any extra wire—and be careful to twist it away from where the tiara will rest on your head.

3. Use the 0.5 mm wire to attach the beads and jewels. This is something you will probably find your own way of doing and you can make up your own designs and formations. However, to make a start cut a fairly long piece of wire— perhaps 20 cm—and thread some beads on to it (odd numbers work well with a big bead in the middle). Position the beads in the middle of the length of wire and make the whole thing into a hoop. Twist the wire ends together a few times and then wind around the tiara band. Squeeze it tight with the pliers to secure.

4. Carry on adding beads and jewels until you achieve the desired effect.

5. Use the Araldite resin to secure any wobbly bits.

6. Wear your tiara with flair and party like a princess!

About Sara

Sara is based in Bristol, and after a brief career in healthcare, is now studying ceramics at Bath University. She has always been creatively inclined and has dabbled in glass, jewellery, drawing, sewing and baking. She has made a series of tiaras using everything she can get her hands on. Sara is a firm believer in the power of craft: "I think in this society of mass production and cheap imports we need to learn/relearn the pleasure of making things with our hands."

Zoé Bibby

BEADY-EYED LIZARD

Bead shops are a bit like sweet shops—millions of little pots of multicoloured seed beads that look good enough to eat. But what can you do with them other than string them up to make a necklace? (Really you shouldn't try to eat them...) How about a cute little reptile that makes both a charming pet and a key ring? This beading will give your hands a bit of a work out...

Materials

+ 1 egg cup of small seed beads
+ 1 m of fishing line

Instructions

1. Hold the fishing line in your left hand (right if you are left-handed) with 5 cm sticking up from your fingers. Thread 2 beads onto the line but do not let them drop below your thumb and finger.

2. Now take the other end of the fishing line in your right hand (left if you are left handed!) and pass the end through the 2 beads in the opposite direction—where the left hand thread is sticking out—and move toward your fingers. Now move your finger and thumb and pull the strings tight so that the beads end up in the middle of the whole length. Steps 1 and 2 form the basic movement, always hold the line in your left hand and cross over with the right.

3. Repeat steps 1 and 2 to form the underside of the lizard's nose.

4. Head: continue to repeat steps 1 and 2 adding the following sets of beads in each movement—3 beads, 3 beads, 4, 4, 5, 5, 3, 3, 3, 3.

5. Front legs: thread 8 beads onto the RIGHT hand line. Missing out the last three beads, thread the right hand line back through the 5 beads closest to your hand. This forms the leg and foot. Now thread 5 beads for the body, as before, threading onto the left hand line and passing the right hand thread back through them. For the second leg, thread 8 beads onto the left hand line and feed the line back along 5 beads, missing out the last 3 beads as before.

6. Body: continue with the basic movement (steps 1 and 2) threading sets of beads as follows—5 beads, 5 beads, 5, 5, 5, 5, 5, 5.

7. Back legs: as for front legs—repeat step 5.

8. Tail: again, continue with the basic movement as follows— 4 beads, 4 beads, 4, 4, 3, 3, 3, 3, 2, 2, 2, 2, 2, 2, 1, 1.

9. Loop: thread 21 beads onto the left hand line, take the end of this line and pass it through the first bead you threaded on of the 21 and pull tight. This will form the hanging loop. Tie a secure knot and pass each end of the fishing line back through the first few beads on opposite sides of the loop.

10. You can now hook your lizard through a keychain, for a funky accessory.

Tips

+ Try using different colour combinations, adding eyes and stripes.

+ The smaller the bead, the smaller the lizard and vice versa. With large wooden beads from a broken car seat cover and garden twine you could have a komodo dragon on the loose!

About Zoë

Zoë is a self-confessed jack-of-all-trades. A freelance artist and maker she comes from a long line of arty folk whose motto/ curse is: "Don't buy one, I'll make you one." After completing a degree in ceramics, Zoë has spent the past 16 years teaching, shopping, travelling and parenting, but always making and creating. She lives in Wiltshire with her husband, two daughters, cats and a room full of junk waiting to be transformed into gorgeous items.

VINYL CUFF

Increase your cool quotient by turning old records into a dashing wrist cuff or a bracelet. Choose an album you love, or make a statement with "Girls Just Wanna Have Fun", or The Bangles. This is a way more interesting way to state your position than slogan tees!

Materials

+ Stanley knife
+ Ruler or straight edge
+ 7" vinyl record (you can use larger but you may have to cut it down to size)
+ Oven mitts
+ A small round jar (spice jars work well)
+ Fine grade sandpaper
+ Clear varnish—either glossy or satin

Instructions

1. Put your oven on to heat up on a low setting—about 100° Celsius should do it.

2. Choose a section of the label that you like (it doesn't have to be the direct centre, but you want it to be across a wide-ish part of the record), and put your ruler along the top edge. Pressing down hard, make four or five cuts, one on top of the other. This should be enough to snap the record in two.

3. Decide on the width you want your bracelet to be—this one is about 3 cm wide—and do the same again, that width down the record, so that you're left with a long, thinnish strip.

4. Your oven should be warmish by now. Take a baking sheet or a piece of foil and place your strip of vinyl on the sheet and insert into the oven. Given the make of the vinyl and the heat of your oven, it might take from a minute to several minutes for it to start melting, so keep checking. You will be able to smell it—a not-so-very nice plastic-y type smell—so be sure to get some ventilation into the room. When it starts to get a bit wavy and warped at the ends, it's time to remove it for shaping. Use oven mitts and caution when removing— it will be HOT!

5. Have something wrist sized in position to shape it, such as a glass jar, smaller for a more wraparound style bracelet, larger for more of a cuff or if you used a larger LP. The vinyl will cool quickly so work with some dexterity here, but don't panic, as you can always reheat it if you want to reshape.

6. Allow it to cool on the jar, and remove it once easy to handle (about 5–10 minutes). Remember, if you're unhappy with the shape, just pop it back in the oven for a minute or so and reshape as necessary. However, too many 'reshapes' and the label can get scorched.

7. Sand the edges, so that they round off a little bit and don't dig into your skin. Don't be too vigorous or you'll sand away your label! We're just cleaning up the edges here and there.

8. Lightly varnish the bracelet on the facing side, using it sparingly on the edges, as they tend to drip (you can varnish the inside to disguise any such casualties). Allow to dry as recommended by the varnish manufacturer.

About Erin

Erin Hensley is a native Kansan transplanted to England and lives with her husband in Bristol. Frugality led her to be creative with gift giving and reusing things she had, or found or took from others' recycling boxes! When not doing strange things with tape measures for her business, Erin Originals, she eats and writes about food, attends gigs and does her best to keep in touch with her huge and far-away family.
www.erinoriginals.com

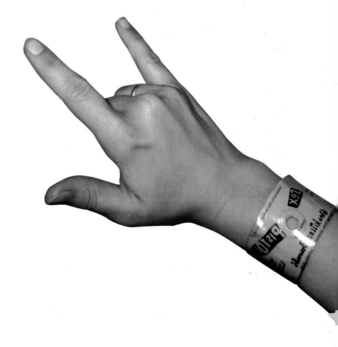

Rob Ryan
PAPERCUT NECKLACE

This intricate necklace is an original pattern by artist Rob Ryan. With a little bit of patience and a steady hand, you can cut it out and wear it to that glitzy premiere, safe in the knowledge that it's strictly limited edition!

Materials

+ Sharp scalpel blades and handle. There are a few different sizes and shaped scalpel handles, try a size 3 (there should be a little number in a circle at the top of the handle). Fit the blade to the handle. A size 10A blade works well. Make sure the blade you get matches the handle design
+ A3 cutting board (optional)
+ A sheet of heavy-ish paper
+ Spray paint

Instructions

1. Make a photocopy of the necklace on the right, enlarging it by 20%. Trace the design onto a sheet of paper. Once you've got the necklace template transferred to the paper of your choice, stick it down onto your cutting board with a few strips of masking tape.

2. Now you are ready to start! It is easiest to start with all the 'holey' bits. Cut out all the middle bits of the chains and the words. Cut out any more small bits that you can and remove the excess paper.

3. Once you've done all of them, it's just a matter of cutting all the way around the edge. If the blade feels like it's dragging, change it for a new one. You should get through about eight blades for something this size. Don't waste your time on blunt blades.

4. Keep going. It will take a while, so you might want to put on some music you like. Take your time, and if you make a mistake, don't panic. Stop, and join it back together with a bit of masking tape and then trim off the excess.

5. Once you've got the whole thing cut out you could spray paint it in a colour you like. If your paper is coloured, this is not essential, but most people have a few unsightly bits of masking tape they want to cover up.

6. To make the clasp work, gently fold the right hand heart in half and slide through the first chain link and then open out again.

Tip

+ Wrap a bit of masking tape around the top of the blade to avoid cutting yourself. It is easy to cut yourself on the top of the blade and since you're only using the tip of the blade to cut the paper, make the rest safe.

About Rob

Rob is an east London based artist working primarily in intricate paper cut outs and illustration. Rob has been interested in drawing since he was a young boy. Every time his dad bought a new shirt, he would give Rob the white card that came inside it to cover with his scribbling. Rob is still doing the same thing; drawing and writing and trying to make sense of things. www.misterrob.co.uk

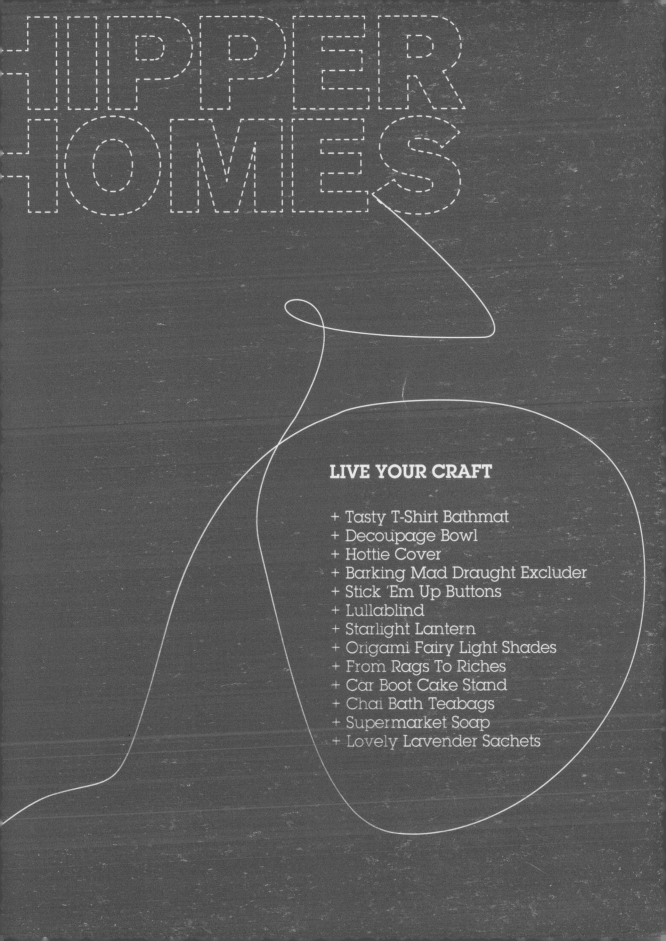

HIPPER HOMES

LIVE YOUR CRAFT

+ Tasty T-Shirt Bathmat
+ Decoupage Bowl
+ Hottie Cover
+ Barking Mad Draught Excluder
+ Stick 'Em Up Buttons
+ Lullablind
+ Starlight Lantern
+ Origami Fairy Light Shades
+ From Rags To Riches
+ Car Boot Cake Stand
+ Chai Bath Teabags
+ Supermarket Soap
+ Lovely Lavender Sachets

Camilla Stacey

TASTY T-SHIRT BATH MAT

This is a great way to put to use all those old band t-shirts you've been keeping because you can't quite bring yourself to throw them out. Okay, so you'll never be able to wear them again, but you'll be able to relive your gig-going past every time you step out of the bath.

Materials

+ One pair of the biggest knitting needles you can get your hands on. This mat was made using some 15 mm plastic needles—but others will do just as well
+ A selection of old t-shirts. 5 XL t-shirts or 8–9 smaller ones. Try to choose colours that match

Instructions

1. First you have to prepare your 'yarn'—the aim is to make one continuous thread of t-shirt material, about 2 cm wide. Using a sharp pair of scissors, cut up about 2 cm from the bottom of the t-shirt, and start cutting around the width of the shirt at a shallow diagonal, so that you are spiralling your way up to the neck. You should end up with one long strip, but don't worry if you've ended up with two or three—you either can sew them together now, or simply knit them in later.

2. Do this with three t-shirts (you can't be sure how many you'll use, so once you've worked your way through the first three you should have a clearer idea of how many more t-shirts to decimate). Roll the resulting yarn into balls.

3. Cast on approximately 30 stitches to your needles—this isn't exact because depending on how big your needles are, and how wide/thick your fabric is you will need a different amount of stitches. What you are looking for here is to cast on enough stitches to make a decent width bath mat.

4. Continue knitting with the yarn until it runs out, or you want to add another colour to the rug. This rug is heavy to knit and you'll probably find that you need to rest it on your lap while you are knitting.

5. To add a new colour in simply start knitting the new yarn in when you reach the end of a row. To secure the new and old yarns you can knot them together at the edge of the row. You will tidy these ends up later.

6. Once you have knitted enough rows to make a mat large enough for your wet feet, it's time to cast off.

7. After you have cast off, go back and secure all those loose ends and snip off any sticky up bits. To secure loose ends, simply weave them into the stitches at the back of the rug: if you want to make your rug extra secure, then using a needle and thread sew down any extra bits.

8. The rug is ready and can be used straight away—it's fully washable at the temperature you would normally wash your t-shirts (you might want to leave one of the labels on one of the t-shirts so you can keep the washing instructions).

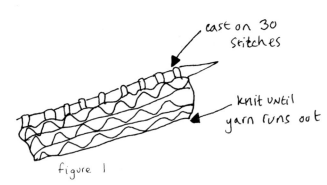

cast on 30 stitches

knit until yarn runs out

figure 1

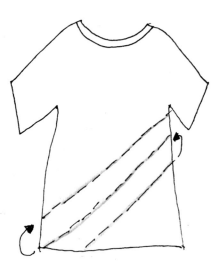

figure 2

About Camilla

Camilla lives in Bristol, studying at art college, and curating shows by emerging artists and craftsters at the Here Shop and Gallery. She has also made a name for herself selling a line of vintage-inspired handmade goods called "Made by Milla", *www.madebymilla.com*. Her work draws on the concept of nostalgia, recycling found objects from previous times in new and witty ways, and reclaiming traditional women's craft skills.

Geraldine Jozefiak
DECOUPAGE BOWL

This is a project anyone can do. Look out for cheap glass plates or bowls, etc., from discount stores. Cut out or tear quality wrapping paper and paste—what could be simpler? This treatment works great on containers, but paper doesn't take kindly to being washed, so keep your project away from water once you've finished.

Materials
+ Glass bowls or plates
+ Wrapping paper with all over design
+ All-purpose glue
+ Paste brush
+ Copy paper
+ Varnish

Instructions

1. Cut into your wrapping paper. Build up a stack of pieces roughly the same size. If you want a more textured look, you don't even have to cut, you can just tear. If you make the pieces too big you'll find them difficult to 'mould' around curves. It's difficult to say how much you'll need. That will depend on the size of pieces you tear/cut, the layers you'll want and the size of your base, but you'll be amazed at how quickly you use them up.

2. Start pasting your paper onto the inside of the bowl. Work with small areas at a time, spreading a little bit of glue, and then sticking the paper on, pattern side up, so that you can see them looking down at the bowl.

3. Paste the pieces as flat as possible to the glass, using your fingers to smooth out any lumps and bumps. Use scraps to fill in any gaps.

4. Turn the bowl upside down, and start doing the same on the outside of the bowl, making sure that the patterned side of the paper is facing you.

5. Varnish the outside in either matt or gloss varnish to secure your paper and paste.

Tips

+ Paper doesn't take kindly to water, so don't wash your bowl once it's finished.

+ You could use the same idea on cheap clip frames. Decide which area of the frame you want to decoupage, dismantle your frame (keep clips safely) and paste. Perhaps you'd like to try fabric scraps on bowls for a more touchy-feely project, or use squares from comic strips for a funky alternative look. You could also use the bowls as 'time capsules' adding names, photocopied photographs, hand-written poems, ticket scraps, coloured papers, etc..

About Geraldine

After training as a primary school teacher, and taking a break to raise a family, Geraldine moved into adult education, She has authored six craft units with the Open College Network and is a craft judge at local and national competitions around the United Kingdom. Geraldine also runs The Craft Teacher Organisation, developing learning resources and training in crafts.
www.the-craft-teacher.com

Erin Hensley
HOTTIE COVER

Keep your tootsies toasty on those long cold winter nights with this fuzzy hot water bottle cosy that can be customised to any variation you wish.

Materials

+ An old jumper
+ An empty hot water bottle, this is for a standard 1.5 litre size bottle
+ Needle and thread

Instructions

1. Choose a sleeve on your jumper, and insert your (empty) hot water bottle from the inside. Adjust the sleeve so that the seam of the sleeve is on the side of the water bottle. If you like, you can fold over the cuff on what will be the neck of the water bottle.

2. Cut a few inches below the bottom of your water bottle. Keep the water bottle in the sleeve so you can follow the slight curve of the bottle when you're cutting.

3. Take the bottle out of the sleeve. This is the point where you'll want to add any embellishing. Use ribbon, transfers, buttons or an appliqué motif, like this bird (see page 25). If your jumper has a pattern, this can be sufficient.

4. Turn the cover inside out and insert the bottle again, again with the seam of the sleeve on the side of the bottle. Using a contrasting coloured thread, sew a loose stitch (also known as a basting stitch). This is just to hold the two pieces together and will be removed later.

5. Carefully remove your bottle from the cover (you'll have to go from the neck end this time, so just roll it carefully over the hottie). Leaving the cover inside out, sew along the guide seam you made in step 4 in a colour that matches the jumper. This is best done with a sewing machine, although it can be done by hand.

6. Remove the basting stitch, trim any excess sweater and threads from the sewn edge, and curl up with your lovely new hottie cover!

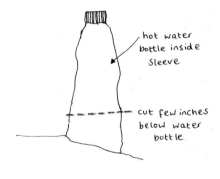

hot water bottle inside sleeve

cut few inches below water bottle

About Erin

See page 61 for bio.

Tip

+ This can be made with a regular jumper, but for a denser effect, try felted wool (see page 24). If you are doing so, make sure to use an extra large sweater, otherwise the cuff will not be big enough to stretch over the bottle.

Camilla Stacey

BARKING MAD DRAUGHT EXCLUDER

This is an environmentally sound way to re-use all those plastic bags you have collected over the years—not only are you reducing landfill by making this super cute sausage creature, but you are helping insulate your house too.

Materials

+ Approx 1 m × 25 cm of reasonably heavy duty fabric—this one was made with an old curtain from a charity shop
+ 20 cm ribbon for trim
+ 3 small scraps of felt or plain fabric in different colours
+ 20 × 10 cm of felt, fur or plain fabric in a contrasting colour
+ Wool yarn
+ Approximately 30 plastic carrier bags
+ Large knitting needle or chopstick

Instructions

1. Fold your fabric so the right side (the side you want to see when the creature is finished) is on the inside and the two long sides are touching.

2. Cut a curved line from point a–b to form the creature's head.

3. Cut a line from point c–d. This will form the creature's tail.

4. Take a length of thread in a colour that matches your fabric sew from point a–x using small stitches and making sure there are no gaps. Sew at about 1 cm from the edge. When you get to point x, make a few small back stitches, to make sure your seam is secure (fig. 1).

5. Do the same with the tail by sewing from point c–d.

6. Do not sew between d and x at this point unless you want a flat inside out creature.

7. Now turn the tube you have made inside out, or rather right side out. Using the knitting needle poke the fabric from the inside to make sure the nose end is nice and pointy and the tail too.

8. Stuff the tube you've made with carrier bags. Start off using one or two scrunched up small to go into the nose and tail, and when you're happy with that, start stuffing with handfuls of bags at a time. It takes at least 30 plastic bags to fill this creature. Make sure you stuff the tail well.

9. You should have a stuffed tube that is pointy at one end, has a tail at the other and a gap between d and x. Fold the edges of the fabric inside around the gap and using matching thread, hand sew the gap closed.

10. If you want your creature's tail to stand up, make a few small stitches in the base of the tail, and a few in the part of the sausage nearest to the tail, and pull gently until it sticks up. Stitch the base of the tail to the back of the creature to hold it at the angle you want.

11. You have made a sausage creature! Now time to give it some features…. Cut two small circles of felt, two medium circles of felt and two large circles—these will make the eyes. Using either glue or hand stitching, put the eyes together and then position on your creature and sew on well (fig. 2).

12. Cut out the ear shapes from felt, fur fabric or contrast material, and attach securely to the creature wherever you think ears should be.

13. Using the wool and a wool needle, sew a nose onto your creature.

14. To finish up you can tie some ribbon around the neck, or perhaps a bow on the tail. Place your creature across the bottom of your door to keep out draughts—or keep it as a strange cuddly toy.

About Camilla

See page 66 for bio.

figure 1

folded fabric
inside out

a.

c. cut out shape

d.

b.   x.

knot

a.

stitch   Back
       Stitch

x.

c.

d.

stuff with
Bags

Sew
closed

SEW on eyes

sew ears onto
body

sew nose with
wool or use felt
instead

figure 2

Victoria Woodcock
STICK 'EM UP BUTTONS

Once you start collecting buttons, it's hard to stop. Luckily, with a little bit of nouse, there's plenty you can do with them. You could put them onto your clothes as a fastening (obviously) or sew them randomly as décor onto bags, t-shirts and what not. Use them as charms on jewellery or slip them onto kirby grips to fasten your hair with flair. But they also make beautiful magnets for haberdashery aficionados.

Materials

+ Araldite glue
+ Little round magnets
+ Buttons

Instructions

1. Glue the magnets to the buttons and leave to dry. Simple as that! Just make sure you glue the non-magnetic side to the button.

DRESSMAKERS 'PIN' BOARD

Organise all your sewing ideas, swatches and so on with your button magnets on this magnetic board that is covered in fabric, but has nothing to do with pins. Chintzy and chirpy, you can knock one up using a cheapo baking sheet and fabric from an old pair of curtains. How very Cath Kidston!

Materials

+ A baking sheet (approximately 28 cm × 35 cm)
+ .5 m of sturdy cotton fabric
+ Needle and thread
+ Fabric glue (optional)

Instructions

1. If your baking tray is raised up slightly at one end, bash (this is the technical term) it flat with a hammer.

2. Cut a piece of fabric that will cover the front and back of the tray allowing enough selvedge to fold over the edges. Wrap the fabric around the board so that the two edges overlap in the middle.

3. Sew up the join. Don't worry about making your stitches neat (this side will be against the wall after all) just try to make it as tight as possible. The way to do this is to push the needle through the fabric on one side (through the right side and out through the wrong side) and then move the needle 1 cm or so away onto the other piece of fabric and make a stitch there (in through the right side and back up through the right side). Then pull tight. Continue in this manner making a stitch every cm or so along the length of the sheet and the fabric should stretch snugly around the board.

4. At each end you should have a several cm of doubled up fabric. Cut away one layer to avoid too much bulk, fold over the remaining layer and attach it to the rest of the fabric using the same sewing technique as before. Fold the fabric at the edges inwards (like when wrapping a present) so that it doesn't show on the right side. Repeat at the other end.

5. To pull the corners taught around the curves: attach the thread to the fabric 2 cm away from the corner diagonally and then push the needle through the tip of the fabric. Pull tight and make similar stitches until the fabric fits the curve. You may need to persevere a little here.

6. You can hang it on the wall now but if you want to cover up all those big sloppy stitches on the back do so with the remainder of your fabric. Cut a piece 1.5 cm bigger than the board all the way around, turn over 2 cm of the edges and iron. Fold the edges diagonally so that they won't show on the right side, iron, and cut any bulk out of the selvedge on the wrong side.

7. A quarter of the way down the material, attach a ribbon or string with a number of stitches at the fold on either side and turn the edges under so they will be hidden.

8. Attach this piece to the board. You can use glue: stick the folded segments to the body of the fabric first, then stick the piece onto the board. But dressmakers in the making can practise their hand stitching by pinning the fabric into place and working an overhand stitch all the way around the edge.

9. Hang, stick on the magnets and get organised.

Tip

+ You could also decorate a baking sheet by sticking a picture to it. But when it says non-stick, it means non-stick. Double sided tape, all-purpose and super glue just aren't going to stay put, so you'll have to sand off the non-stick surface if you're going down this route.

Li Jonsson
LULLABLIND

So you've forgone curtains for the cleaner lines of roller blinds. Fresh and minimalist yes, but perhaps a little impersonal? Not these ones. Every time you pull them down, they sing you a little lullaby. So get your jammies on and try this quirky little project on for size.

Materials
+ 1 roller blind with a side fitting
+ 1 hand cranked music box (you can get them off e-bay)
+ 5 × 5 cm L-brackets
+ Pliers
+ Hammer
+ File
+ Nuts and bolts
+ Screwdriver
+ Drill (optional)

Instructions

1. The blind will come with two side fittings. Attach an L-bracket with a nut and bolt in the lower hole of one of the side fittings, as illustrated in fig. 1.

2. Take the hand-cranked music box and snap off the end of the handle (the bit that turns to the side). File down the bit that remains, so that it is square rather than round at the end (fig. 2).

3. Attach the music box with a nut and bolt to the L-bracket, making sure the squared-off leftover from the handle is centred in the hole. Note: you might have to loosen the nuts slightly to centre the squared-off handle. When it is centred, don't forget to tighten the bolts up again.

4. Make a small hole in the plastic that holds the blind up. You can do this by either drilling, or simply by hammering a small nail into the plastic. The hole does not need to be more than 1 cm deep, and should be smaller than the thickness of the leftover bit of handle.

5. Add the two pieces together by hammering the music box fitting into the hole of the blind. Since the hole is small and round, the squared off metal handle will create a grip in the plastic when forced in (fig. 3).

6. You can now put your blind up. Start with the side which does not have the music box attached.

7. When you have finished, you will notice that you can control the speed of the tune by pulling the string. When you pull it gently, the tune will sound perfect. So slow down your pace and let the lullablind sing you to sleep.

About Li

Li comes from Sweden and moved to the United Kingdom to do her undergraduate degree in design at Goldsmiths. She has worked for design agencies including Curro Claret, Rainer Pehl and Punk Royal. She believes that craft and design have the unique capacity to be both fun and political, and embraces the growing interest in DIY culture: "Through making, the consumer is no longer a passive target, but instead becomes an active and engaged actor in a consumer society."
www.lovli.co.uk

figure 1

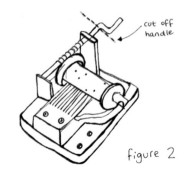

cut off handle

figure 2

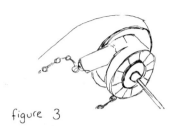

figure 3

Mark Butcher
STARLIGHT LANTERN

Here's a lesson straight from the school of Habitat: a chic urban table lamp from the most utilitarian of materials. This 12-point star lantern will put your powers of 3-D construction to the test and take you back to the classroom to get your hands covered in all purpose glue.

Materials

+ 36 willow sticks— approximately 35 cm long
+ 5 A3 sheets of white wet strength tissue paper
+ A roll of masking tape
+ A set of 10 or 20 fairy lights
+ Large bowl
+ All purpose glue
+ Sponge
+ Wire cutters

Instructions

1. Prepare all of your materials and lay them out in front of you.

2. Take two willow sticks and a piece of masking tape approximately 10 cm long. Stick the tape around one end of the willow stick, so the sticky sides of the tape stick together and a long section of the tape remains. This method of sticking is called 'flagging'.

3. Take the other willow stick and wrap the trailing piece of tape around the end of the other stick. Keep wrapping it around both sticks in an irregular pattern until the join is tight and secure.

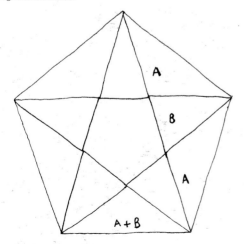

4. Join three other sticks in the same manner to form the shape of a pentagon star, remembering to flag every stick as you secure it to the other. The neater and tighter the joins the better the result of your lantern will be.

5. Once you have a pentagon star shape you need to start thinking in 3-D. In the centre of the star you will see the shape of a pentagon. Five of your willow sticks will need to run through the middle of this pentagon and meet in the middle. Flag sections of tape to secure these sticks together where the sticks cross over one another and where the ends meet. Then flag the side of the willow at the end of the sticks, where they cross over, at each corner of the pentagon.

6. After this stage you should be able to imagine your lantern in 3-D. From each of the willow sticks you need to repeat this pentagon star until all your willow sticks have been used, always remembering to flag the tape to the sticks.

7. Take the first light on the string of fairy lights and position it in one end of the lantern star's points. This will be where the lead appears out of your lantern. The rest of the lights should be evenly rigged within the lantern frame: stretch the lights from one corner of the lantern to the other until they are all used, attaching them with thin strips of masking tape.

8. Cut the tissue paper into A5 and A4 sized pieces (or US letter if you're across the pond) and then mix equal amounts of all-purpose glue and water in the large bowl. Lay the tissue paper onto a smooth surface. Dip the sponge into the glue, mix then wipe the sponge over a single sheet of tissue paper until it is wet through.

9. Carefully lift the sheet of tissue paper off the smooth surface with both hands and lay it over the lantern frame. Continue this process until the entire lantern is covered as neatly as possible. Don't worry if the paper seems a little baggy—as it dries it will become taut.

10. The sponge can be used to dab glue on any little bits of paper that are sticking out.

11. Leave the lantern to dry overnight. Don't turn your lights on until it is completely dry!

Tip

+ You can use this process on any lantern frame. Once you've mastered the technique you can experiment with building weird and wonderful shapes.

About Mark

Mark has always been involved in the arts in some context. His t-shirts are for sale in American Retro, and his illustrations have featured in *Graphic Magazine, Kill Pop, Don't Magazine* and on banners in clubs across London. He also designed the cover for *Dress Up Jonaflid*, the first album of his partner, Jonathan (*www.myspace.com/markaflid*). Mark currently works in film, and lives with Jonathan in South London. His work can be viewed on *www.markfuatch.moonfruit.com*.

Hannah Ayre
ORIGAMI FAIRY LIGHT SHADES

A traditional Japanese lily design slotted over fairy light bulbs makes a lovely mellow glow and adds a touch of class to your old fairy light chain. The ones pictured are made from white office paper, but you can use coloured paper or old magazines. They are safe to use at home, but fairy lights are not the most reliable of lighting apparatus, so don't leave them on overnight or when you go out, just in case.

Materials

+ Several sheets of 21 × 21 cm paper (or A4 with a bit chopped off)
+ Fairy lights

Instructions

1. Working on a flat surface, fold a piece of paper in half, bringing the opposite corners together, then unfold. Repeat in the other direction.

2. Fold in half yet again, this time bringing the straight edges together. Open and repeat in the opposite direction. This time do not open out but with the paper folded take hold of the folded edge and tease the central crease on both sides outwards. You should now have a 3-D star shape. Flatten to create a triangle. You should now have two flaps pointing to the left and two to the right.

3. Keeping most of your model flat on the table, lift one flap upwards, so it is at a right angle to the rest of the model.

4. Separate the two layers of this flap by placing a finger or pencil inside. Squash this cone shape flat, so that the centre fold meets with the centre line across your square.

5. Repeat step 4 for the remaining three flaps. Arrange the flaps so that there are two on each side and there is a short gap down the centre.

6. Bring the raw edges of the uppermost flap to meet the centre line, crease, and then unfold them.

7. Now lift up the straight edge, which runs across the centre of the model. Bringing just the first layer of flaps from the left and right to meet in the centre. Press everything flat so that you now have a small kite shape on top of a larger one. Fold the central triangular flap in the opposite direction so that it faces the same direction as the open points.

8. Repeat step 7 four times, with the four sections of the model.

9. Arrange the flaps on your model so that the plain smooth faces are visible.

10. You should have a diamond shape. At one end the points will be open (these will become petals). At the other end they all meet. From this end, fold the edges into the centre, so that they meet on the central line. Repeat on all four sides.

11. You are nearly there. Open the model up a little by putting your hand inside the open end. You should now see the four petals. Using a pencil, curl the end of the petals around it outwards.

12. Cut about 2 mm off the point end of your lily. Insert a pencil to open the folds a little. Place over your fairy light. If you have any trouble getting your flowers to stay on, a little blue tac should do the trick.

Tip

+ It is generally easier to fold the paper away from you. Origami can be a bit tricky, so try not to be put off if you don't get it right the first time.

About Hannah

Hannah is an Edinburgh based environmental artist, and has been creating things from scrap for as long as she can remember. Using mostly reclaimed materials, she has created objects that range from home crafts to large-scale outdoor sculpture. In addition to her art, she also works in education with schools, galleries and environmental organisations, teaching and inspiring people about arts, crafts and environmental issues.
www.photobox.co.uk/hannahpalindrome@yahoo.co.uk

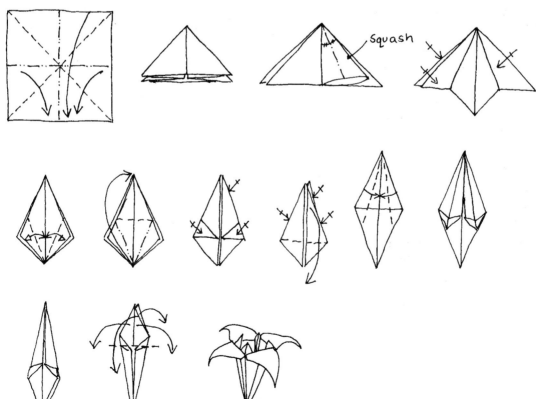

Squash

Tajender Sagoo
FROM RAGS TO RICHES

Recycle your fabric scraps into shabby-chic placemats with this simple, basic weaving technique. Strips of fabric (or plastic or paper) are fixed down lengthwise. These are known as 'warp' strips. A further set of strips are woven under and over the warp strips, and these are known as 'fill strips' (or weft strips to some).

Materials

+ A piece of sturdy rectangular cardboard
+ Old rags shredded into long 1–1.5 cm wide strips
+ Masking tape

Instructions

1. Cut a rectangle of card slightly larger than you want the finished placemat to be. Along the shorter edges, mark 1 cm intervals and cut a 1 cm deep slit at each point (fig. 1).

2. Take a length of rag for the warp and start wrapping the rag across the length of the card using the slits to hold the warp in place. Keep the tension of the warp even—not too tight or you will bend the card. If you come to the end of a warp rag, simply tie on another end to it. (Alternatively to avoid lots of knots, cut a longer strip using the same technique as for the Eco Shopper page 46. Remember to cut vertically).

3. When you have wound a warp onto the whole card you can start to weave. The technique you are going to use is called a 'plain weave'.

4. At one end, use your fingers to lift up every other warp thread and pass a fill rag between the two sets of threads, from left to right at a right angle to the warp. When you have gone all the way across the warp, use your fingers to push the fill rag down evenly so it lies straight across the warp.

5. Now bring the fill back across the warp from left to right lifting up the alternate set of warp threads and passing the rag fill through the warp. Be careful not to pull the yarn too tight or you will distort the warp and end up with wavy edges on the placemat. Again, use your fingers to beat down the fill.

6. Repeat steps 4 and 5 until you have worked across the length of the card. When you come to the end of a fill thread just start with another. You can knot them together or overlap the ends in the warp.

7. Tidy any loose ends by sewing them into the back of the cloth.

8. Place sticky tape at both ends of the cloth to keep the fill from moving. Cut the warp off the card down the middle of the back. Hand or machine-sew a line at both ends, removing the sticky tape. Alternatively, you can knot the warp ends together in pairs. Neatly trim the warp threads.

Tips

+ Experiment with different colours and textures of fabric for the warp and fill threads. As well as using rags you can try plastic, paper or thin wooden strips in the fill.

+ Make a giant rectangle from a cardboard box and weave a rug in the same way.

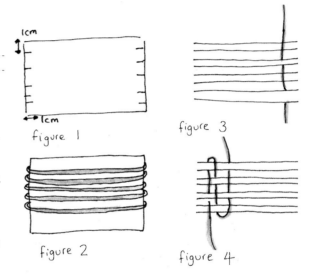

figure 1

figure 2

figure 3

figure 4

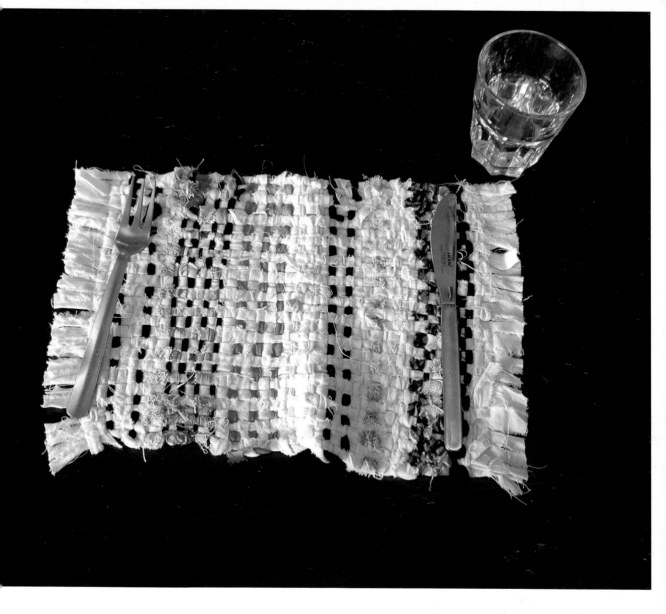

About Tajender

Tajender is a visual artist working with textiles, photography and weaving. As a child, growing up in east London, she was surrounded by the vibrant colours and textures of fabrics from all corners of the earth. It was therefore no surprise when she went to study textiles at Central St Martins School of Art. As well as focussing on her art she also offers lessons in weaving. "You don't need expensive equipment to weave simple things, just time", she says, "and you will always make something unique."

Victoria Woodcock
CAR BOOT CAKE STAND

If you've got the group heading to your place for a craft-a-thon,
a clothes swap or a spot of Bingo then let them eat cake off this
vintage cake stand. Stand back and see if anyone notices that
it actually consists of three plates and two sherry glasses
bought on the cheap at the local car boot!

Materials

+ 3 plates of varying size
+ 2 sherry glasses (tall shot glasses
  or egg cups will also do)
+ Araldite glue
+ An orange stick or matchstick
+ Set of compasses
+ 2 paperweights, or other small
  heavy objects

Instructions

1. Give your crockery and glassware a good clean and dry
   it thoroughly.

2. Place the plates face down on a piece of pa   nd draw
   around them. Cut out the paper circles nd   into quarters
   to find the centre.

3. Using a ruler, measure the diameter of t   sherry glass' rim.
   Set a compass to half the resulting meas   ment and draw
   a circle in the centre of the paper circle: he large and
   medium sized plates.

4. Repeat with the glass's base measur   (this should be a
   larger size than the rim) on the paper   es of the medium
   and small sized plates.

5. Cut out the circles from the rim measrem   ace the paper
   circles on top of the respective plates and ma   t the centre
   circles faintly in pencil. Cut out the bae circles (u is is the
   first circle on the little plate template and the sec ond on the
   medium plate template) and draw them onto t'ne underneath
   of the plates.

6. Mix up the glue with a matchstick and carefully run a thin
   layer around the lip of one glass rim and place it onto the
   pencilled circle on the top of the large plate. Place a little
   paperweight, or other small heavy object on top of the glass
   and leave to dry. Repeat with the medium plate. Refer to the
   glue instructions as to when the glue has dried, be brave and
   pick up the plate holding the glass. If it falls apart, glue again
   with a slightly thicker layer of glue.

7. Glue the base of the glass on the largest plate to the circle on
   the bottom of the medium plate. Place the weight on top and
   leave to dry. Finally stick the small plate onto the base of the
   second glass. Leave to dry for a day or so before you use.

8. Whip up some cupcakes with candy coloured icing to adorn
   your masterpiece.

Tip

+ If all the measuring sounds a bit too complicated, you
  can stick the glasses to the plates using guesswork. But be
  warned; if the glasses are off-centre, the cake stand can
  look a little odd.

Susan Beal
CHAI BATH TEABAGS

So you drink tea in the morning do you? Susan Beal recommends you bathe in it instead. Forget the PG Tips and opt for a more fragrant blend by mixing green tea and spices and stitching it up in little cloth teabags. Apparently, tea is a great remover of stinks from your feet—and undoubtedly all other bits of your body—so these easy-to-make bath treats are the perfect gift for your smelly, yet elegant, friends! Give them a whirl yourself: run a hot bath and pop a teabag under the stream of water—it's Chai charming!

Materials

+ Stapler
+ Glue
+ 3 tbsp loose green tea
+ 1 tbsp cinnamon
+ 1 tbsp ginger
+ 1 tsp cardamom
+ 1 tsp cloves
+ Remnant of white cotton fabric—try using an old (but clean) pillowcase
+ White string
+ Colourful felt squares
+ Old tea tin or box

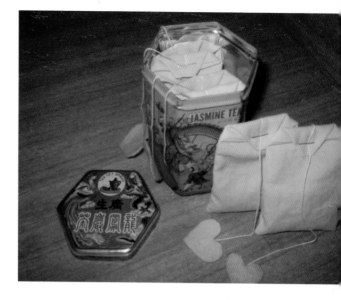

Instructions

1. Combine the tea and spices in a bowl and set aside.

2. Cut out four pieces of fabric 8 × 10 cm. Fold one in half so it's 4 × 5 cm. Stitch up each side with a running stitch close to the edge.

3. Turn the bag right side out and spoon a quarter of the tea and spice mixture into it. To close up the bag, fold over the upper corners so that they join in the middle, making a point. Fold down the tip of the point. Fold the top section over the body of the bag (fig. 1).

4. Place a 15 cm piece of string over the top of the bag so that it sits in the centre on both sides. Hold the bag closed and the string in position with your fingers.

5. Staple the fold down, catching the string with it on both sides of the bag.

6. Repeat to make the other three teabags.

7. Cut out small felt hearts (or any shape of your choice) and use a small dab of glue to attach them to the end of the string. Leave to dry.

8. Package them in a box or tin and give them to someone you like!

figure 1

About Susan

Susan Beal (also known as Susanstars) loves crafting with recycled and vintage pieces. She lives with artist husband, Andrew, in Los Angeles and Portland, Oregon, and writes about art and craft for *Cutting Edge, Adorn, Craft, Bust, ReadyMade,* and *Venus.* She also runs a monthly "West Coast Crafty" column on www.getcrafty.com. Susan's first book, *Super Crafty* (co-written with her PDX Super Crafty collective) was published in 2005, and she's working on a new jewellery-making book for spring 2008. She sells her work on www.susanstars.com.

Dr Sara Robb
SUPERMARKET SOAP

Without any special ingredients or equipment, you can make luxurious scented soaps in your own home. Most soap making books get bogged down in formulations and saponifications (technical terms!). Here the chemistry has been done for you—all you have to do is follow the steps, just like you would if you were baking. The only important thing is that you must get the measurements in tables 1 and 2 precisely right, otherwise it won't work.... It's a piece of cake!

Materials

+ Scales
+ Timer or clock
+ Rubber gloves
+ Large glass jar (a large instant coffee jar works well)
+ Small plastic or glass bowl
+ 2–4 litre plastic container with lid (an empty ice cream tub works well)
+ Wooden spoon
+ Large metal whisk or electric hand blender
+ Microwave oven
+ An old towel
+ Caustic soda (also known as lye, sodium hydroxide or NaOH— available from some supermarkets and most DIY stores)
+ Water (still bottled, or rain. Tap water is not recommended, but can be used)
+ A selection of oils totalling the recipe weight for each column (See Table 2)
+ Selected additions (See Table 3)

Making the Lye Solution

The lye solution (caustic soda in water) is the potion that converts the oil to soap. The chemical formula in a nutshell is that sodium hydroxide (the chemical term for lye) reacts with the oil to make glycerine and soap. During this process, all the lye is consumed and therefore is eliminated from the soap, leaving the gentle glycerine and soap molecules behind. Lye is a chemical, so make sure that you read the safety warning on the label before you embark on this little adventure!

Table 1 outlines the amount of water and caustic soda used in this method. It is imperative that the quantities used do not deviate from those specified in the table.

TABLE 1
Lye solution

Water	250 grams
Caustic soda	125 grams

1. Gather the following: rubber gloves, water, caustic soda, large glass jar, small plastic or glass bowl, scale, wooden spoon, and the timer.

2. Place the large glass jar on the scales. If they are digital scales, set them to zero, to eliminate the jar weight. Alternatively, note the weight of the jar.

3. Weigh the water into the jar so the water weight is 250 g. If you haven't set your scales to zero, the weight on the scale will be the jar weight plus 250 g.

4. Put the jar of water to the side and put on your gloves.

5. Place the small plastic or glass bowl on the scale and either reset the scales to zero, or calculate the weight of the bowl as you did in steps 2 and 3. Carefully pour the caustic soda into the bowl until you have 125 g of caustic soda.

ALWAYS ADD THE CAUSTIC SODA POWDER TO THE WATER NEVER ADD WATER TO CAUSTIC SODA!

6. Place your water jar in the sink. Slowly pour the caustic soda into it. You can swirl the jar to begin mixing the caustic soda into the water.

7. After you have added all the caustic soda, use the wooden spoon to stir it in. You may wish to have a dedicated spoon for mixing lye, rather than a spoon contaminated with cooking odour (the odour might transfer from the spoon to your lye and into your soap... onion-scented soap is not very desirable).

8. Continue to stir until there are no crystals floating in the solution. As the caustic soda dissolves into the water, the solution will heat up, eventually reaching approximately 90° Celsius. Leave the jar in the sink to cool for 30 minutes, so that it cools to approximately 50° Celsius (no need to measure the temperature as this does not need to be precise). Make sure it is out of reach of children and pets. While the lye solution is cooling, get the oils and additions ready.

Selecting and Mixing the Oils

The Supermarket Soap method requires you choose one oil from EACH column. The oils in Column A are liquid at room temperature and are the base of your soap recipe. Column B oils are also liquid at room temperature. Column B oils are more exotic oils that will give your soap different qualities and colours. Finally, the oils in Column C are solid at room temperature and in general help to make the soap hard. The qualities of the soap will change with the oils you select. You can experiment with various combinations. The only rule is you must select and use 350 g of oil from Column A, 250 g of oil from Column B and 400 g of oil from Column C. Do not change the weights of each specified columns or the formula will not work.

TABLE 2
Choose oils from each coloumn and add by weight

A	B	C
Olive Oil	Sweet Almond Oil	Coconut Oil
Soy Oil	Sunflower oil*	Lard
Peanut oil	Hazelnut oil	Vegetable Shortening
Safflower oil	Hemp Oil	
Corn Oil	Avocado Oil	
Sunflower Oil*		
350 grams TOTAL	250 grams TOTAL	400 grams TOTAL

*You will note Sunflower Oil is listed in Column A and Column B. This is the only oil which appears in two columns and can be used as either a Column A oil or a Column B oil.

Appropriate oil mixtures would be:

Column A	Olive Oil	350 grams
Column B	Sunflower Oil	250 grams
Column C	Coconut Oil	400 grams

OR

Column A	Sunflower Oil	350 grams
Column B	Sweet Almond Oil	250 grams
Column C	Vegetable Shortening	400 grams

9. Select the oils from Table 2. It is necessary that all ingredients be measured by weight. Be sure you have enough of each oil. When weighing water, 500 ml weighs 500 g, so a 500 ml bottle gives you 500 g of water. But oil weighs less than water and so a 500 ml bottle will be less than 500 g. Many of the oils in Column B are available in 250 ml bottles. As this will end up less than 250 g, you will need to buy 2 bottles (you have your trusty scales, so don't worry, this isn't as complicated as it sounds!).

10. Gather the following: oils, scale, plastic container, microwave safe bowl (if the plastic container is microwave safe, you can use this), and hand blender or large whisk.

11. Place the plastic container on the scales, and re-zero them (or measure the weight of the container, as in steps 2 and 3). Pour the Column A oil into the container until you have 350 g.

12. Reset the scales to zero, and pour 250 g of the Column B oil you selected into the container. You now have a total of 600 g oil in the container.

13. If your container is microwave safe, reset the scales again and add the Column C oil to the container until you have 400 g. If your container cannot be placed in the microwave, weigh the selected Column C oil, the solid oil, into a separate microwave safe container.

14. Place either your container of mixed oils or your container with just the Column C oil into the microwave and microwave on medium power until the oil is melted. The reason to melt this solid Column C oil is to ease the mixing with the liquid Column A and Column B oils.

15. Stir all oils together well using either a hand blender or whisk.

16. Your oils are now ready to go. You should have a plastic container with 350 g Column A oil, 250 g Column B oil, and 400 g Column C oil. This plastic container will serve as your soap mould so there will be no need to transfer the oils to an additional container.

Optional Additional Ingredients

Unscented soaps, without additions, are ideal for babies and for people with fragrance sensitivities. If this is what you're after, skip directly to the Making the Soap section. If you want something a bit smelly and a bit luxurious, the key will be essential oils or fragrance oils. These are available from chemists (note: these may not be suitable for babies, pregnant or lactating women). Alternatively spices and teas can add a more subtle fragrance. Honey will give the soap a light sugary smell and add moisturising properties. You can add more than one of the listed additions to the Supermarket Soap base. Be creative and have fun choosing your additions. There are endless combinations to choose from!

TABLE 3
Luxury oil additions

Additive	Amount	Quality
Essential oil	Up to 1 tbs	Fragrance
Fragrance oil	Up to 2 tbs	Fragrance
Honey	Up to 1 tbs	Emollient
Food Colouring	Up to 1 tsp	Colour
Spice Powder *	1 tsp	Colour & Fragrance
Herbal Tea †	1-2 sachets	Colour, Fragrance & Texture
Rolled Oats	1-2 tbs	Texture
Grated Beeswax	10 grams	Emollient
Grains, Seeds, Rice Powder ‡	Up to 1 tbs	Exfoliating

* (such as cinnamon, ginger, turmeric or nutmeg)
† (such as chamomile, elderflower, blackberry or dandelion)
‡ (these can add texture to create an exfoliating bar)

17. Select the additions you wish to add to the soap and have them ready to add to the soap mixture. It is recommended that you use a tablespoon of a Column B oil to suspend essential oils or fragrance oils. The additions are the only ingredients used in Supermarket Soap which do not need to be measured by weight. You can experiment with different quantities and combinations.

Making the Soap

You now have all the ingredients you need to make Supermarket Soap. You have your oil mixture, the lye solution, which has been cooling for 30 minutes or more and you have gathered the additional ingredients you would like to add. Now time for the easy bit... making the soap!

18. Gather the oil mixture, lye, additions, hand blender or whisk, gloves, the lid to your container and the old towel. Put on your gloves.

19. It is time to begin adding the lye solution to the oil mixture. Slowly pour the lye solution into the container containing the oil mixture while stirring. If you are using the stick blender, stir without using the power until you have added all the lye solution. The lye solution will mix with the oil even though one is water and one is oil. This is because the oil has begun to be converted to soap and glycerine.

20. Once all the lye has been added to the oil, set the empty jar in the sink. It is now time to really stir. If you are using the electric hand blender, begin to stir the soap on low speed. If you are using a whisk, stir continuously. The raw soap solution will thicken as you stir, as the lye converts the oil to soap and glycerine. If you are using a hand blender, the raw soap will thicken more quickly than if you are stirring by hand. When this 'batter' begins to create lines that trace the path of where you have stirred, it's time to stir in the additional ingredients.

21. If you are using an electric hand blender, stir without using power. Mix the essential oils or fragrance oils thoroughly into the soap mixture. With the other ingredients, such as spices, seeds or tea, you can try various methods. You might mix them through the soap mixture, mix them partially through for a swirl effect or sprinkle them on top.

22. Cover the soap by placing the lid on your container, and wrapping the container in the old towel. You may have noticed that the soap mixture warms up as the oil is converted to soap by the lye. The soap will continue to heat up and thicken. This is the chemical reaction occurring. It's like putting a cake in the oven, except that the heat occurs naturally. The soap will continue to warm, and as it does so it will gel together. This is a result of the lye chemically processing the oils into soap. This will take a few hours to complete. You can peek to make sure the soap is gelling.

23. Check your soap after an hour or two. You will be able to see the progression of the gel from the centre to the edges of the soap as it heats up and then the solidification as the mixture cools from the edge back to the centre.

24. Let your soap sit overnight, snugly tucked up in its container and towel.

25. The following day, you can unwrap your soap and see the final product. The soap should now be very solid. Ease the sides of the container away from the soap slab. You should be able to turn the soap out of the container. If not, place the container in the freezer for 15 minutes and try again. Cooling the soap container will help release the soap.

26. Cut your soap into desired shapes and sizes.

27. Let the soap cure for a few days or weeks. During this time, water will evaporate from the soap and it will become harder. Congratulations, your Supermarket Soap is finished —now scrub up!

Tips

Some recommended combinations for your soap

+ Lavender Chamomile Soap
  Oils: A. Olive, B. Sunflower C. Coconut
  Additional ingredients: 1 teaspoon lavender essential oil,
  2 sachets chamomile tea, a little red and blue food colouring

+ Avocado Soap
  Oils: A. Sunflower, B. Avocado, C. Lard
  Additional ingredients: 1 tablespoon Fragrance Oil

+ Summer Garden Soap
  Oils: A. Sunflower, B. Sweet Almond, C. Vegetable shortening
  Additional ingredients: 2 sachets rose and raspberry herbal
  tea mixed into batter, 1 tablespoon lilac fragrance oil,
  1 sachet rose and raspberry herbal tea, sprinkled on top

+ Nut and Honey Soap
  Oils A. Groundnut, B. Hazelnut, C. Coconut
  Additional ingredients: 1 tablespoon crystallised honey,
  1 tablespoon ground cinnamon, 1 teaspoon ground nutmeg

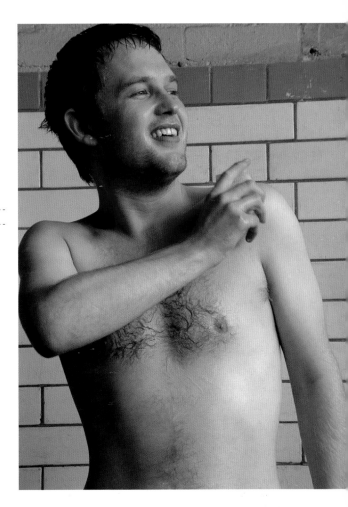

About Dr Sara

Dr Sara Robb grew up in the American Midwest and moved to Britain in 1998 to take up a post-doctorate fellowship in neuroscience. She began making soap after the birth of her daughter Jasmine, and founded the company Bath Potions (*www.bathpotions.com*). Her products have been featured in fairs around the world, and on Channel 4's *Big Brother*. She also teaches classes, including "Bath Potions with Dr Sara".

Betsy Greer

LOVELY LAVENDER SACHETS

It's a well-known fact that crafty folk hate waste—turning rubbish into designer goods—that's what it's all about! So what about the bits and pieces of yarn hanging around from all your wonderful knitting projects of days gone by? Betsy Greer turns the leftovers into nifty little squares, which can be sewn together into a quilt, a scarf, or in this instance, fragrant lavender sachets to make all your handmade goods smell like they've just come out of an expensive designer store.

Materials

+ Leftover yarn
  (preferably non-chunky)
+ Knitting needles to match
  the thickness of your yarn
+ Muslin bags with drawstring
  (buy them from craft stores or
  sew them yourself)
+ Fresh lavender
+ Small crochet hook or yarn needle
+ Stitch holder—or a big safety pin
+ Button (approximately 1 cm in
  diameter)

Instructions

1. Cast on 21 stitches. The size of your pouch will depend on the thickness of your yarn and the size of your needles.

2. Work in stockinette stitch (knit 1 row, purl 1 row) until you have a square or a swatch about 9 cm long.

3. Bo all 21 stitches.

4. Repeat steps one and two with the same yarn and start to make a button hole tab: bo 7 stitches, place the next 7 stitches on a stitch holder, bo the last 7 stitches. Cut the yarn with a 15 cm tail to weave in later.

5. With the right side of your knit facing you (that's the side with the 'V' shapes) put the stitches on the holder back onto a knitting needle. Start at the left-hand side so that the point of the needle is on the right-hand side. Thread the end of the yarn from the ball through the yarn needle and attach it to the back of the knit (the bumpy side) by threading it through a few stitches, just underneath the stitch closest to the needle point.

6. Work with these 7 stitches in stockinette stitch for 4 cm.

7. Starting on a knit row, work the buttonhole as follows (see page 22 for buttonhole help):
   + Row 1: k2, bo 3 sts, k2
   + Row 2: p2, co 3 sts
     (using Cable Cast on method: page 23), p2
   + Row 3: k
   + Row 4: p2tog, bo remaining stitches

8. Join the two squares together. Place the cast-on edges together, pin and connect the three sides without the button tab. You can do this with a crochet hook—pulling the thread through the inner part of the knit stitches and over the edge. Or use a mattress stitch to join the side seams (worked on the right side of the fabric) and a back stitch to join the cast on edges (worked on the wrong side of the fabric).

9. Sew the button onto the front of the bag—making sure it fits in the buttonhole first.

10. Fill a muslin drawstring bag half-full with fresh lavender (pick it from your neighbour's garden if needs be), secure the drawstring tightly, place in the remaining open side of the pouch and fasten button.

About Betsy

Betsy believes in the power of craft for political good. "Craft has been a part of society since its inception.... The moment you make something yourself instead of buying something premade, you are subverting the status quo." She loves small joys, big dreams, soy products, leg warmers, 80s nostalgia, bad television, Lionel Ritchie and making things. One day she wants to live in a cottage by the sea filled with yarn, pets, love, books, laughter and cake.

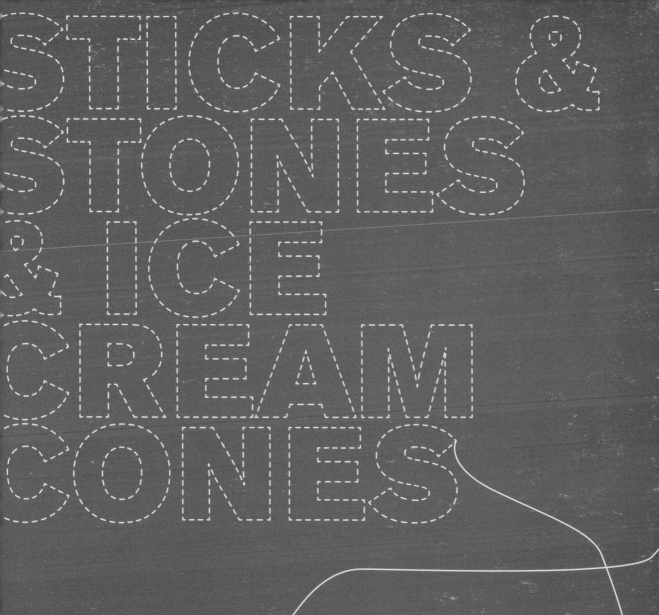

STICKS & STONES & ICE CREAM CONES

THE RANDOM BITS THAT FILL THE GAPS

+ Fabulous Fleecy Felted Flowers
+ Jumper Monkey
+ Record Breaking Notebooks
+ The Gin Binger's Booze Cosy
+ Aye-Aye-Sailor i-Pod Cosy
+ Recycled Tie Purses
+ Antenna Tag
+ Puppet Junkie
+ Nara Paintchip Passport Holder
+ Hipster PDA

FABULOUS FLEECY FELTED FLOWERS

This idea uses hand felting as opposed to machine felting—a similar process, but better for really delicate creations like these dazzlingly colourful flowers. Think of them as fleece onions, with a major wow factor.

Materials

+ Pre-dyed fleece in a variety of colours. Merino fleece is cheap and easy to work with. You can buy this at craft shops or online
+ Large bowl, soap and hot water
+ Wire and masking tape
+ Scalpel or sharp knife

Instructions

The flower head

1. You will be working from the centre of the ball outwards. Pull some loose fibre apart and between the palms of your hands, roll it into a ball. Aim for a golf ball size to start with.

2. Pick a different colour and carefully cover your ball with thin strands of fibre building up a layer in a crosshatch pattern (this will help the fibres to felt together). It's a good idea to make a rough plan on paper of the order you want you colours to be in. You are aiming to cover the ball completely with an even layer about 1.5 cm thick.

3. Keep adding more and more colourful layers, being careful to keep it in a ball shape as you go. Layers don't have to be just one colour—mix it up a bit if you like, especially on the last (outside) layer. When you are happy with the size, you are ready to wet it. Bear in mind your ball will end up at least 40 per cent smaller after you've felted it, so make it quite big to begin with.

4. Hand felting: Gently sprinkle hot water (as hot as you can stand it—use rubber gloves if necessary) evenly on the ball whilst turning it in your hands to maintain the shape. Apply a bit of soap in the palm of your hand and start to smooth the outer layer. Bit by bit, add more water until the whole ball is saturated. The skill is to do it gradually, if you end up with a big soapy soggy mess you've gone too far! Gently rub the fleece to agitate the fibres. This will encourage them to knit together. As the ball becomes more compacted, you can get a bit rougher with it, roll it around on a flat surface if you like. Take the opportunity to exorcise that pent up frustration—it's quite cathartic!

5. When it's too hard to squeeze anymore and it has shrunk to less than half the original size, it's ready (this should take about 30 minutes). If your ball is a particularly big one then once the outer layers are felted tightly enough you can cheat and finish it off in the washing machine on a quick wash. Otherwise, rinse the soap out and leave to dry.

6. Now the exciting bit—brace yourselves! Slice that furry geode open and marvel at the wonder within.

Petals and decoration

7. If you've got this far having mastered felt making in 3-D, then making a flat piece to cut your petals out of will be a walk in the park. Applying the same basic principles, layer up loose fleece (crosshatch) to about 4 cm thick. Remember, the main surface you will see will be the front and back so pay particular attention to the first and last layer you put down.

8. On a flat surface, wet the sheet, gently drawing the fibres from the outer edge in. When it gets compacted enough, get rough with it, it can take it. When you can't pull it apart anymore it's ready.

9. Let it dry and then cut the petals out, they can be any shape you like—be creative.

10. Sew or stick the petals on. Apply the odd bead here and there to make it super-cute and the flower head is done!

The stem

Now there's no getting away from the fact that the stem is a bit trickier to master so if you're all felted out, sew a pin on the back and call it a brooch! For those of you made of stronger stuff—here goes.

11. Make a stem (about 50 cm) from some sturdy wire or use several strips of wire taped together if you've only got the thin and flimsy stuff. It's got to hold the weight of your fabulous flower head so if you're not a Nobel prize winning physicist and calculations are not your forté then don't worry—the worst that can happen is you end up with a species called Gravitious Floppious (Latin obviously).

12. Using the wire at one end, form a coiled bowl shape for your flower head to sit in. Consider the size as this will be covered in felt and you still need the flower head to fit snugly into it. Tear off little pieces of masking tape and cover the entire stem as if you were using papier mâché.

13. Because this is a fairly awkward shape, it's not easy to cover the whole thing in a dry layer of fleece before wetting it. Starting at one end wrap dry fleece around the stem and gently wet it down and add dry fleece on top as you go. The water and soap will act as a kind of glue. However, it is very important to not let the fleece felt before adding more dry fleece, otherwise it will not knit together.

14. When the whole stem is covered in an even layer of wet fleece, start to felt it together in the same way you made the other bits. Gently squeeze out the water and re-apply hot water if necessary. The felt should follow the contour of the stem so use your fingers and thumbs to mould it into shape. Then all that's left to do is stitch the stem to the flower.

Clarity Miller
JUMPER MONKEY

These cute little apes have so much personality you can't help but love 'em—maybe that's why they're so popular at the moment. Clarity Miller has been making them long before the fad caught on, so take some tips from the original and best.

Materials

+ 1 old stripey jumper— preferably wool
+ 2 buttons
+ Fibrefill or other stuffing
+ Hand quilting thread and a needle

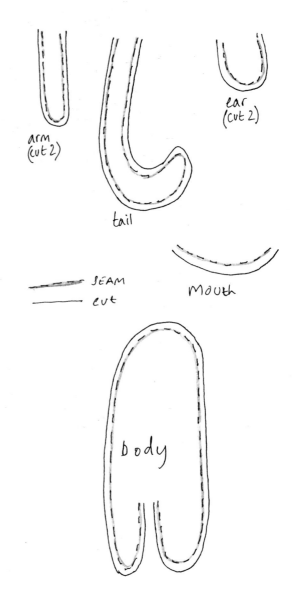

Instructions

1. Make a pattern using the rough guidelines on the right. Feel free to improvise!

2. Turn your jumper inside out and pin the pattern parts onto the wrong side of the fabric. Draw around the pattern pieces and mark on the dotted lines. Remember to repin and draw the ear and arm pieces.

3. Place some pins in the middle of the shapes to hold the two layers together and cut them out. Sew along the dotted lines with a sewing machine or by hand.

4. Remove the pins and turn the pieces right side out. Stuff the body, arms and tail, leaving about 2 cm at the top of the arms and tail.

5. On the body, whip stitch between the legs, folding fabric under as you go (see page 26). Take a doubled piece of thread or yarn and tie it around the torso, creating a head for your monkey.

6. Folding the raw edges of fabric under, whip stitch the mouth onto the head, adding stuffing as you go. Attach the ears, arms and tail, folding the raw edge underneath. Sew on button eyes, or embroider them on with a bit of black thread.

Tips

+ The pattern and instructions do not have to be followed exactly. Variation makes your monkey unique. Add lots of stuffing for a chubby monkey; make his tail extremely long so he can hang from branches; make an outfit out of felt for him! Be creative and make your monkey your own.

+ Throw some dried beans or pulses in with the stuffing for the beanbag effect.

About Clarity

Clarity Miller has been crafting ever since she figured out how to sew a leotard for her Cabbage Patch doll. A long illness when she was a teenager meant that she had plenty of time on her hands to sew, and she began making all her own clothes. After graduating from a degree in photography, she went back to her seamstress roots, and now works in fashion and sells her clothes and jumper monkeys on *www.blackbirdfashion.com* and *www. buyolympia.com.*

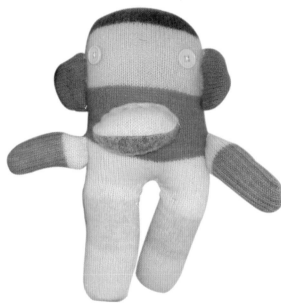

Tara Bursey
RECORD BREAKING NOTEBOOKS

These little record sleeve notebooks are a modern twist on bookbinding. Using the Coptic stitch—a time-honoured yet basic bookbinding technique—they are the perfect creative outlet for the crafty rock 'n' roller. They are a cheap, clever and striking alternative to ordinary notepads, and make fantastic customised gifts for your music loving friends.

Materials

+ 1 record sleeve
+ About 30 sheets of the A4 paper of your choice (graph paper, lined paper, plain paper, coloured paper, Japanese/Thai tissue… whatever your little heart desires)
+ Coloured embroidery thread, or doubled up polyester thread
+ Sewing needle
+ An awl or a comparable tool sharp enough to poke small, clean circular holes through the record sleeve (a plain old flat-headed nail will do the trick just fine)
+ A pair of scissors or a good utility knife

Instructions

1. To start, you need to cut out a front and back cover. Using a pencil and ruler, draw two 11 × 14.85 cm frames around the areas of the sleeve you would like to serve as your cover images. Cut the covers out cleanly and carefully with a sharp knife or scissors.

2. Next you will need to prepare the pages of your notebook. Cut or tidily tear 30 sheets of A4 sized paper (21 × 29.7 cm) in half horizontally, into 21 × 14.85 cm sheets. Fold each of the cut sheets vertically (short side to short side) and group them into booklets of five sheets. You will end up with a total of six booklets comprising five folded sheets each.

3. The next step is to poke holes in both covers and in each booklet through which you will sew all of the components together. 1 cm from the left side of the front cover, mark six points, 1.5, 3 and 4.5 cm from the top, and 1.5, 3 and 4.5 cm from the bottom (fig. 1—overleaf). Repeat the process on the inside back cover (fig. 2). Once you've marked each point, pierce them carefully (taking care not to crease or bend your cover) with the tool of your choice.

4. Open each of the six booklets of notebook pages and mark the same points (1.5, 3 and 4.5 cm) along each of the booklets' inside folds (fig. 3). Pierce through the marked points, this time with a sharp sewing needle. When you are finished, sandwich the six booklets in between the front and back covers. This will give you an idea of how the finished notebook will look. Check the spine of the book at this point: all of your holes in both covers and all of your booklets should line up perfectly with one another.

5. You are now ready to bind your notebook! Prepare a length of thread (approximately 1.5 m) in the colour of your choice. Starting with the first hole on the top of your first booklet, use the Coptic stitch to bind the first booklet to the front cover, each booklet to the next, and the back cover to the rest of the bound book.

Coptic Stitch

The Coptic stitch was originally developed in Egypt during the second or third century AD. It is a simple bookbinding method characterised by its exposed stitching along the spine that resembles a crochet stitch. The Coptic stitch is durable, functional and after a bit of practice, is surprisingly simple to execute.

6. Holding the front cover and one of the booklets of paper together in one hand, stick the needle through the first hole at the top of the booklet. Leave a tail about 8 cm long inside the booklet, which you will eventually tie secure. Then put the needle into the first hole in the front cover, (the hole in the cover next to the hole in the booklet you just emerged from) and push it into the space between the front cover and the booklet. Insert the needle back into the hole in the booklet you originally entered through, (fig. 4—solid lines are visible on the OUTSIDE; dotted lines indicate what is going on INSIDE the booklet).

7. Now that you are back inside the booklet and have completed one stitch, tighten in a bit while making sure your tail doesn't escape though the hole. You will want to tighten the stitch enough that the tension is firm, but not so tight that you run the risk of tearing or expanding the holes in your booklets, or your book will not open properly.

8. Insert your needle into the second hole in the first booklet and repeat the same process, sticking the needle through the outside of the second hole in the cover, between the cover and the booklet, and back through the second hole in the booklet. Repeat this until you have stitched all six holes along the first booklet and cover.

9. Once you have reached the final hole, instead of re-inserting the needle back into the final hole in the booklet from between the booklet and cover, insert it into the last hole of a second booklet, directly below the first booklet. Continue stitching back in the other direction along the second booklet in the same manner you treated the first, except this time when you bring the needle up through each hole in the booklet, loop the needle around the stitch holding the first booklet to the cover (fig. 5).

10. Repeat this same process until you have reached the last booklet. At that point, you will attach the back cover the same way you attached the front cover.

11. Tie off your two ends inside the first and last booklets with a double knot to the adjacent secure stitches.

12. Voila! You have a finished notebook. Rock 'n' write to your hearts content.

Tips

+ If it takes you a few tries to perfect the stitch or complete an entire book, fear not! Many find the Coptic stitch a little difficult at first, but rest assured, it gets easier with practise and persistence. There are also plenty of fantastic websites on the Coptic stitch you can consult for additional help and information.

+ As you become more comfortable with the Coptic stitch, you can try making books that are as large and as thick as you want.

+ If you are using American letter sized paper it is slightly 'shorter' than A4. In that case the folding of the paper is exactly the same but you will need to cut the covers to 11 × 14 cm.

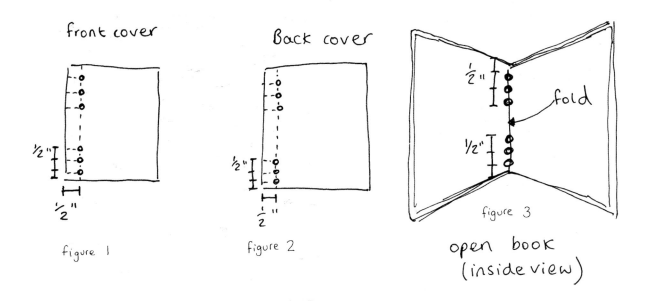

front cover

figure 1

Back cover

figure 2

fold

figure 3

open book
(inside view)

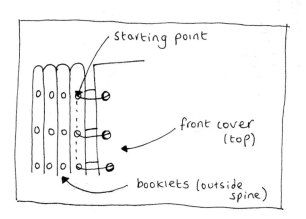

starting point

front cover
(top)

booklets (outside
spine)

figure 4

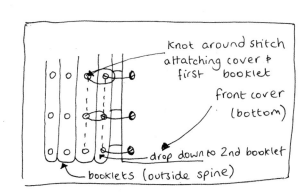

Knot around stitch
attatching cover &
first booklet

front cover
(bottom)

drop down to 2nd booklet

booklets (outside spine)

figure 5

About Tara

Tara Bursey is a long-time zine writer, vinyl enthusiast, do-it-yourself-er and punk rocker. She is also a visual artist whose diverse practice encompasses sculpture, installation, drawing and craft. Her most recent projects include an artist's talk entitled "Zines: A Short History of the Underground Publication" and a solo exhibition, *White Wash*, which employed both found, fabricated and altered institutional garments as a means of addressing the constructive/destructive nature of systems. In addition to her work as a fine artist, Tara operates actively within Toronto's independent music and small press communities as a DJ, writer, illustrator and designer. She currently lives and works in Toronto, Canada.

Victoria Woodcock
THE GIN BINGER'S BOOZE COSY

Much better than a brown paper bag and hipper than a hipflask. Grab a bottle of gin and think of Miss Hannigan. Yes, the dastardly orphan keeper from *Annie* might have been a mean old spinster, but she sure worked that gin chic. The French knickers, the feather boa, the dishevelled hair, the bath paddle... if only she'd had one of these natty bottle covers.... "We love you Miss Hannigan!"

Materials
+ An unwanted sock
+ Needle and thread
+ Scraps of felt or t-shirt material
+ A 35 cl bottle of hard booze

Instructions

1. Choose your sock. You want one that has a bit of stretch left in it so it will hold your bottle snugly.

2. Wiggle the sock over your bottle of choice so that the ribbing comes up to the neck. Mark where the bottle's base is on the sock (this should be just above the heel) and take the bottle out. Snip straight across the sock just below the mark. Turn the sock inside out, and sew a gently curved line to close up the gap. Try it out for size.

3. That's pretty much it, but some stitchin' will make your booze look even more bitchin'! To add your initials to your tipple draw the letters in chalk onto the felt. Cut them out, dab them with a glue-stick and position them on your cosy whilst it's over the bottle.

4. You can appliqué any shape you like. For the unicorn photocopy the shape, cut it out and draw around it on the felt.

5. Now stitch into place—see page 25 for details.

Tips

Some other great things about the booze cosy!

+ If you're wearing gloves ('cause we know all the alkies come from cold climes) this reinvented sock will give you some traction on your beloved bottle.

+ For all you cheapskates—no one will discern that you're swigging cheap own-brand instead of Gordon's.

+ Since socks come in pairs you can make a matching one for your drinking buddy.

AYE-AYE-SAILOR I-POD COSY

Oh how we have lost the tactile charms of buying and listening to music—the scratchy sound quality, the sensuous joy of flipping through vinyl, the weight of the record as it slips out of its cover... These days the download rules, but keep the touchy-feely vibe alive with this distinctly low-fi knitted cover. It will protect your i-Pod from scratches, and keep your tunes warm at sea.

For rookie knitters, this may be a gruelling workout, so read this pattern through and study the how to knit section at the front of the book—then get stuck in!

Materials

+ 1 ball of worsted weight yarn in blue, white and navy
+ Size 3.5 mm knitting needles (or size needed to obtain gauge—see page 19)
+ Yarn needle
+ Gold button with an anchor on it
+ Needle and thread (white)

Instructions

Gauge: 25 stitches and 36 rows = 10 × 10 cm in stockinette stitch.

1. Knit up a test square and calculate your gauge. This quick i-Pod knit is a great way to get to grips with gauges, as you want a snug fit.

Knit the front

2. Cast on 20 stitches in blue. Work 6 rows of stockinette stitch (knit 1 row, purl 1 row).

3. Switch to white yarn and work a further 6 rows in stockinette.

4. Knit a further three stripes in this way.

5. With the sixth stripe (white) knit the first 5 rows in stockinette but instead of purling the 6th row, knit it. Switch to blue and knit two rows. Knitting each row results in a garter stitch— a good way to finish as it ensures the edge won't curl up. Cast off 20 stitches.

Knit the back and the flap

6. Cast on 19 stitches and follow the instructions for the front but complete all 6 rows of the 6th stripe in stockinette.

7. Switch to the blue yarn and knit the flap in garter stitch. Slipping the fist stitch on every row will result in nice neat edges, so from here on knit every row as follows:
   + Row 1: sl1 k18
   + Row 2: sl1 k18
   + Row 3: sl1 k1 sl1 k1 psso k11 k2tog k2
   + Rows 4, 5 and 6: sl1 k16
   + Row 7: sl1 k1 sl1 k1 psso k9 k2tog k2
   + Rows 8, 9 and 10: sl1 k14
   + Row 11: sl1 k1 sl1 k1 psso k7 k2tog k2
   + Rows 12, 13 and 14: sl1 k12
   + Row 15: sl1 k1 sl1 k1 psso k5 k2tog k2
   + Row 16: sl1 k10
   + Row 17 (button hole): sl1 k3 cast off 3 k4
   + Row 18: sl1 k3 co 4 (use cable cast on—see page 23) k4
   + Row 19, 20, 21 and 22: sl1 k10
   + Cast off 11 stitches

8. On the centre of the back piece, below the flap, duplicate stitch the anchor from the chart. Start at the bottom and work your way across and up row by row.

9. To assemble the cosy you will join the two side seams using mattress stitch (see page 20). Line up the stripes and gently pin the two edges together. Start at the bottom and work the mattress stitch, removing the pins as you go. Remember to work on the right side. To seal up the bottom, turn the cosy inside out, line up the two cast on edges, pin and use a backstitch to sew the two sides together.

10. Weave in the ends and attach the button.

Tip

+ If the stripes are a stitch out, undo a couple of stitches and on the side where the stripe was lower just pass the needle under one bar instead of two and then continue to catch two bars and the stripes will pull together perfectly.

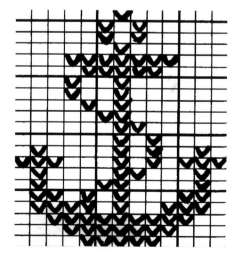

Hannah Ayre

RECYCLED TIE PURSES

This idea was conceived while rummaging round opportunity shops (charity shops) in Australia. They are handy for carrying money, make-up, jewellery and other bits and bobs.

Materials

+ Tie (the wider the better)
+ Button
+ Needle and thread
+ Embroidery thread

Instructions

1. The largest point of the tie will become the flap of the purse. Decide how deep you want your purse. Do this by folding a small section of the tie upwards to meet the large point. At the point where the tie starts to taper, fold it back on itself away from the point. Where the length of the tie meets the folded edge you have created, cut off the remaining length of the tie—i.e. cut approximately 30 cm from the large point of the tie. This could be longer if you want to create a glasses or i-Pod case.

2. Fold the cut end inside itself halfway up the length of the rectangular part of the tie. With the seam of the tie facing upwards, fold the straight edge up to where the tie begins to taper to its point. You have created two pockets for the purse. Put your fingers inside them. With some ties the lining bunches up at this point and needs to be removed before you can continue. You may need to re-stitch the seam of the tie when you do this.

3. Reverse the fold, so that the seams are showing on the outside. Stitch along the two outside edges. It is best stitched by hand rather that machine, as you can sew closer to the edge.

4. Turn your purse inside out (or rather the right way round). Fold the point downwards to create a flap.

5. Create a loop to go around the button from the embroidery thread. Do this by taking a length of the thread approximately 40 cm long. Thread it onto a needle. Tie both ends in a knot together. With the needle, catch a piece of fabric on the inside of the flap, right by the point. Your needle should come out at the point. Pull all the way through, so that the knot meets the fabric. Twist the needle so that the thread twists tightly. With your forefinger and thumb take hold of the thread and let it twist back on itself so that it looks like rope. When doing this, ensure that 3 cm of thread is left at the needle end which doesn't twist back on itself. This gives you space to catch the fabric with the needle just next to the knot.

6. Thread your needle though the end of the loop you have created. Cut off the needle and tie the end of the thread in another knot.

7. Sew on your button where this loop meets the front of your purse. Iron the purse and off you go!

About Hannah

See page 78 for bio.

ANTENNA TAG

Kids—graffiti is cool! Hit up your hood with your own distinctive tag—your neighbour's car is a good place to start.... And what's more, if you follow the Knitta Please steps to becoming a graffiti artist, you're sure not to get in trouble. Welcome to the soft, colourful, outlaw world of knitted graffiti, "warming the world one car antenna at a time...". The original knitting graffiti crew, Knitta Please, say: "By tagging with our colorful knitted pieces we not only intend to soften vandalism methodology but also encourage dissenting actions that can be beautiful."

Materials

+ Acrylic, worsted weight yarn (two colours for the zigzag pattern and as many as you like to make stripes)
+ 5 mm knitting needles
+ Yarn needle
+ Small piece of cardboard
+ Hole punch
+ Dark coloured hooded top to wear when tagging!

Instructions

1. Calculate your gauge—it's not too vital, but there should be around 20–26 stitches in a 10 cm area—don't worry about the rows, you can just knit until it is the correct length.

2. Cast on 10 stitches and knit 4 rows (NO PURL). Then work in stockinette stitch until the piece measures around 70 cm in length. Finish with 4 knit rows.

3. Pin the two sides together to form a tube. Cut a length of yarn and join using the mattress stitch (see page 20).

4. Take a piece of small card and draw on your own distinctive tag. Make a hole with a hole-punch at one end and slip a short 15 cm piece of ribbon or yarn through it. Attach it to your knitted tube.

5. Wearing appropriate clothing, slip out under the cover of darkness and tag a car, (preferably one that you can keep under surveillance to observe the owners face when they see your tag) and slip it over the antenna.

6. Take a photo of your handiwork and email it to: hello@knittaplease.com.

Pattern variations

7. Make stripes by using a different coloured yarn when you feel like it (see page 19).

8. More confident and experienced knittas can try their hand at a zigzag pattern:
   Key: mc = main colour, sc = second colour
   Cast on 10 stitches as before.
   K 4 rows mc (no purl) then begin pattern.
   + Row 1: k 2 mc, add sc k 4, k 4 mc
   + Row 2: purl same stitches and colours
   + Row 3: k3 mc, k4 sc, k3 mc
   + Row 4: purl same stitches and colours
   + Row 5: k 4 mc, k4 sc, k 2 mc
   + Row 5: purl same stitches and colours
   + Row 6: k 3 mc, k 4 sc, k 3 mc
   + Row 7: purl same stitches and colours
   + Row 8: k 2 mc, k 4 sc, k 4 mc

Repeat these 8 rows to desired length, end with 4 knitted rows.

About Knitta Please

Knitta Please began like a rock and roll band. At a Tuesday night knit jam AKrylik and PolyCotN were discussing their frustration over unfinished knitting projects: half-knitted sweaters and balls of yarn gathering dust. They knitted their first doorknob cozy and then it dawned on them... a tag crew of knitters, bombing the inner city with vibrant, stitched works of art, wrapped around everything from beer bottles on easy nights to public monuments and utility poles on more ambitious outings. Today, Knitta is a group of 11 ladies of all ages, races, nationalities, religions, sexual orientation... and gender. Their plans include tagging other countries and encouraging new groups to form, worldwide. www.knittaplease.com

Seif al'Hasani
PUPPET JUNKIE

Puppets make perfect friends; they never talk back or embarrass you in public. They have lots of sharp, rusty points and so are ideal for self-defence. Not to mention the fact that they will instantly mark the owner out as an individual of taste, a true patron of avant-garde arts!

Materials

+ Drill
+ Saw
+ Screwdriver
+ Cutting pliers
+ Soldering iron
+ Vice (to secure the body while drilling and gluing)
+ Screws
+ Araldite glue
+ Steel wire
+ Junk of every possible description

Instructions

1. Gather together your junk. Every puppet is different and there is no systematic approach to making them, it really depends on your design. Below is a list of just some of the materials you could use:

   Body: Drift wood (for that nice, weathered look), tape cassettes, wooden ruler, vintage metal boxes, mouse traps, etc..

   Limbs: Chains, springs, large sewing needles, keys, steel wire, safety pins, rope and pulley hooks. These are readily available at any hardware store.

   Heads, eyes and mouths: Buttons, beads, table tennis balls, dice, little light bulbs.

   Accessories (for decorating the body): Stamps, vintage photos and stickers, cut-out illustrations, vintage coins, fabric.

2. Start by laying out the different parts on the workspace. It will be much easier if you can see how it all fits together before you start.

3. Measure the diameter of the limbs and with the body in the vice drill holes at the sides of the body; make sure the holes are the same size as the limbs. You need one hole for each limb and the head (if your design has got one!).

4. Mix up the two-part glue (follow the instructions on the label carefully) and use a matchstick to place some in the drilled holes. Insert the limbs in place, it is important that you keep it still while the glue is drying. Follow the instructions on the label for how long you should leave it to dry.

5. Finally; add accessories as you see fit. Wrap lengths of steel wire around the body and limbs to move the limbs.

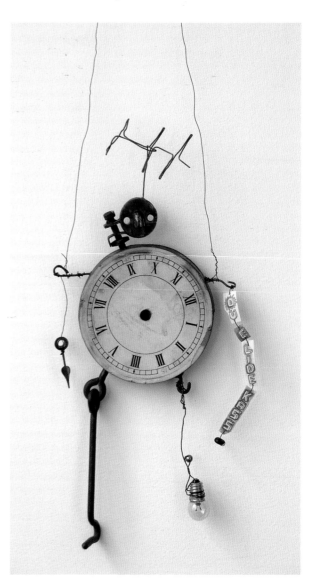

About Seif

For Seif crafts are all about self-sufficiency and being able to produce what you need, rather than getting it from the supermarket like everybody else. Family and friends are the inspiration for his puppets. He uses a combination of found objects, printed ephemera and his own illustrations to try to express an individual's character traits and unique personality. www.block214.com/index.html

Narangkar Khalsa

NARA PAINTCHIP PASSPORT HOLDER

Hit your DIY superstore and make off with a stash of paint swatch strips to make a fantastic travel wallet. Insert your passport, arrive at the airport approximately four hours early, remove your shoes and belt, discard your drinking water and nail clippers into the proper receptacles, and remember you are the most fashionable international traveler in line for the strip search.

The dimensions of this pattern are measured to fit an average passport booklet of 8.9 × 12.7 cm.

Materials

+ Basic sewing machine (this pattern is too thick to sew by hand)
+ 1 leather needle for your machine, and good quality thread
+ Craft knife
+ Stainless steel straight edge
+ Masking tape
+ Glue suitable for paper
+ About 4 or 5 similarly hued paint swatches that measure at least 21.25 cm long: these will be for the 'warp' direction of the booklet
+ About 4 or 5 paint swatches in complimentary shades that measure at least 15 cm long: these will be for the 'fill' direction of the booklet
+ 4 complementary hued paint swatches at least 6.3 cm × 15 cm for your pockets: don't cut these into strips!

Instructions

1. Cut the 'warp' and 'fill' paint swatches lengthwise into 1.25 cm strips with your craft knife and straight edge. Be careful not to tear them!

2. Line up your long warp strips to form a 15 cm wide block. Make sure you have no spaces in between, and that the top ends are lined up evenly. Secure them in place with masking tape to your work surface. Place the tape about 5 cm from the top edge.

3. Weave in one fill strip across the very top edge, push up to the tape and place glue on every alternating strip that will be the 'under' side of the fill. Now slide your fill strip over the glue and gently lift up the 'over' edges, put dots of glue and press down. Wait for your glue to dry.

4. Weave in your fill strips, using colours that you think look nice and complement your warp colours. What you get is a pretty grid or spectrum depending on your intentions. Make sure your fill strip in the middle is at a perfect right angle, so it folds in half without too much trouble (fig. 1).

5. Place dots of glue on the ends of the middle fills to ensure a little more stability and reduce wear and tear. Once down at the end of the warp, glue the last fill strip down just as you did with the top one. Place the whole thing inside a thick book so it dries flat.

6. Once it has dried, trim off all the loose ends of the fill strips (ideally with a guillotine, but scissors will do fine).

7. Fold at the centre before you start to sew the pockets on. Cut your pocket paint swatches to size—you want two on each of the 15 cm sides.

8. Before you sew everything together, add any mbellishments to your passport holder. Weave in a satin ribbon along the middle with the end of a safety pin to act as a bookmark (fig. 2).

9. Place your booklet opened up flat with the inner side facing up and the pockets lined up so that the bottom pocket sits about 1.25 cm from the fold and the top pocket is about 2.5 cm away from the bottom pocket.

10. Start your seam, using about a 3 mm seam allowance, at one corner and stitch all around the perimeter. Trim all rough edges and threads (fig. 3).

About Narangkar

Narangkar is a fine artist who lives and works in Oakland, California. She creates paintings, collages, basketweaves and needle-works and uses these traditional mediums to express non-traditional, figurative ideas that stem from her life experiences. In 2002, she started to work with the idea of random colour palettes and began weaving colour samples through one another in a basketweave pattern. This creative concept expanded to embrace functional art objects, such as passport holders and wallets.
www.narawallets.com

figure 1

figure 2

figure 3

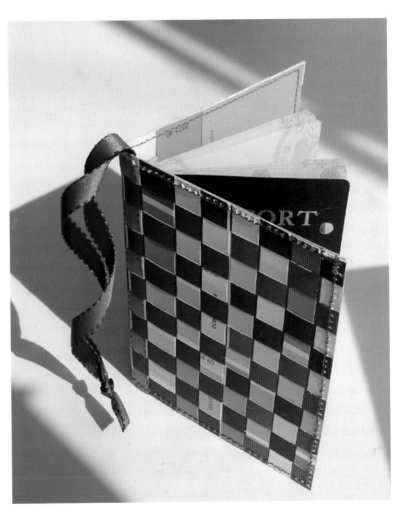

figure 4

Susan Rowe Harrison

HIPSTER PDA

If you fall into the technophobic category of craftster, then you'll know what it feels like to miss a meeting thanks to an incomprehensible electronic PDA. So go back to basics with this simple HPDA (Hipster PDA), which is basically a stack of index cards held together with a binder clip. You can easily add/purge cards from the stack, and pimp it up as you desire…. No bookbinding techniques required!

Materials

+ Screw post (also called Chicago post, binding post or interscrew— available from craft shops and office supply retailers). The shaft diameter should be 5.5 mm— the size of a standard hole punch
+ Drill (manual or electric)
+ Binders board, cardboard, or even thin sheets of wood
+ Pack of index cards—lined, grid or plain—whichever you prefer
+ Pretty wrapping paper, magazine pages, fabric, wallpaper or any other decorative surface to cover your PDA with
+ Thin card, or light plastic —to use as dividers
+ Rotary cutter (optional)

Instructions

1. Cut two pieces of your binding board or alternative stiff material that you have chosen to the size of your index cards (roughly 7 × 13 cm—see fig. 1).

2. Cut your covering material (wrapping paper, fabric, etc.) approximately 2 cm wider on all sides than your binding board (fig. 2).

3. Place the board in the centre of the covering material, mark the corners in pencil and glue the material to the board.

4. Flip the board over, so that the material side is facing upwards, and place a clean sheet of paper over it. Smooth out any wrinkles with a spatula or another wide, flat implement. Smooth from the centre outwards.

5. Do the same with the back cover.

6. Cut a small V shaped notch out of each corner, and glue down the outer edges of the covering material (fig. 3).

7. If you want that shiny professional finish, use a contrasting fabric or paper, to paste on the inside, covering up the edges of the cover (figs. 4 and 5).

8. Allow the glue to dry. This can take 12–24 hours depending on the type of glue.

9. Once the glue has dried, sandwich the index cards in between the cover boards, and clamp all the layers together.

10. Mark a point approximately 2 cm from the corner of the block, and using a drill bit that matches the shaft diameter of your screw post (usually 5.5 mm), drill a hole through the whole darn thing.

11. Insert your screw post, and get serious!

Tips

+ Use a rotary cutter to perforate the edges of some of the index cards, so that you can tear them off easily.

+ If you want to cover your notebook with raw wood, Perspex, vinyl or an album cover, skip steps 1–7.

figure 1

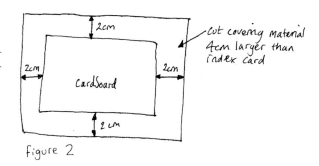

figure 2

About Susan

Susan is an artful crafter and a crafty artist, living in Toronto. She avoids the art vs craft debate by incorporating aspects of each into the other. Her work has been exhibited in North America, Asia, and Europe, and can be seen on:
www.lunule.blogspot.com

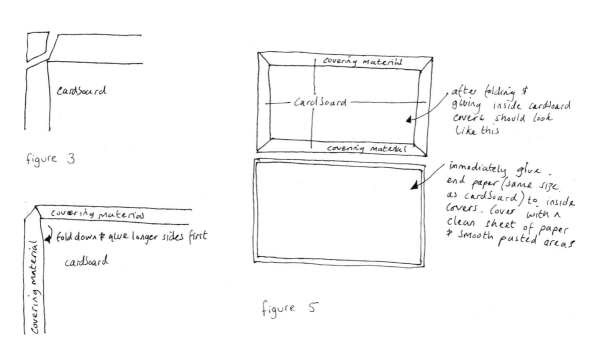

figure 3

cardboard

covering material

fold down & glue longer sides first

covering material

cardboard

figure 4

covering material

cardboard

covering material

after folding &
gluing inside cardboard
covers should look
like this

immediately glue
end paper (same size
as cardboard) to inside
covers. Cover with a
clean sheet of paper
& smooth pasted areas

figure 5

SMALL WONDERS

THINGS TO MAKE
FOR AND WITH KIDS

+ Horsing Around Sock Puppet
+ Hedgehog Puppet
+ Hanging in the Balance
+ Curtain Spiders
+ Jackito-Lanterns
+ Steiner Dolls
+ Beeswax Candles
+ Abbey Baby Bib
+ Pixie Bonnet
+ Frock Rocking in Smocking
+ Umbrella Shadow Show
+ Eco Warrior Kite

Tratincica Slavicek

HORSING AROUND SOCK PUPPET

Your dear old woollen socks got shrunk in the wash—and besides, they have holes in the toes…. What a joy to turn them into horses, giraffes, aliens, or who knows what else! Children, particularly little ones, love these 'chewing' types of puppets and get a thrill out of putting their fingers in the puppet's mouth!

Materials

+ 1 old sock
  (well washed before use)
+ Knitting yarn
+ 2 buttons
+ Small square of felt
+ Cardboard
+ Piece of foam rubber
+ Yarn needle
+ Sewing needle
+ Sewing threads in
  matching colours
+ All-purpose glue

Instructions

1. With a pair of scissors, trim a piece of foam rubber into a semi-oval shape (leave one side flat) that fits well inside the heel of the sock.

2. Turn the sock inside out and glue the foam oval (the curvy side) into the heel. Turn the sock the right way round, and you have the horse's forehead.

3. Cut your cardboard into a narrow rectangle the length from the heel to the opening of the sock. You are going to use this to make the horse's mane.

4. Wrap the yarn around the cardboard until it is covered (fig. 1). Trim the end and tie the yarn to itself to make it secure.

5. Thread another piece of yarn onto a yarn needle and loop it under four or five strands in the middle of the cardboard at one end. Pull half the length of the yarn through and tie the two ends together in a knot. Repeat the same procedure, slipping the needle under a section of yarn and tying the ends, along the length of the cardboard—you're basically sewing the yarn to secure it (fig. 2). Make the last knot a double one.

6. Turn over the cardboard and cut the yarn through the middle (fig. 3). You should end up with an oblong pom-pom—a sort of long woolly caterpillar. Give it a bit of a shake to straighten.

7. Sew the mane along the middle of the sock from the top of the padded heel area (the horse's forehead) towards the sock opening.

8. Sew two buttons onto the forehead for the eyes.

9. Fold a piece of felt in half and cut out two ear-shaped pieces (they should be roughly pie shaped when unfolded). Fold the ear shapes in half and sew them onto the sock on either side of the mane.

10. Push the toe-area inwards to form the mouth and put your hand in the sock so that your thumb is in the lower jaw and your fingers in the upper jaw. Try out the different faces the horse can make!

Tip

+ Experiment with felt and bits of wool to make some tasty vegetables to feed your horse!

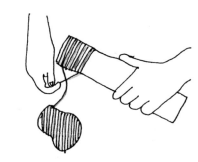

figure 1

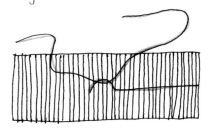

figure 2

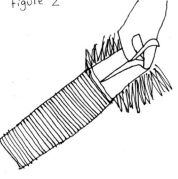

figure 3

Tratincica (Tinka for short) was born and raised in Croatia. She worked for a long time as a pre-school teacher, and children remain a great source of inspiration for her art, craft and puppetry ideas. Tinka moved to England in 2004, and became a freelance puppeteer. She finds it hard to keep her hands still; almost without noticing, crafty creatures are taking over her house, crawling over every available surface...

HEDGEHOG PUPPET

Pom-poms are fun to make with kids and with a little extra effort you can bring a fluffy ball to life as a hedgehog puppet.

Materials

+ Knitting yarns in different shades of "hedgehog colours"
+ Cardboard cut into two rings
+ Piece of felt or some soft sweater material
+ Stuffing—woolly bits and leftovers, cotton wool or white stuffing
+ Thread in matching colour to felt
+ Thick black thread for the nose
+ All purpose glue
+ Buttons or beads for eyes
+ Wooden stick for handle
+ Crochet hook (optional)

Instructions

1. Cut two CD sized, donut shaped rings out of cardboard and put the rings one on top of the other.

2. Cut several 1 m long strands of thin yarn in different shades, and join them together to make one thick, multi-stranded yarn. Start winding this around the double cardboard ring (fig. 1).

3. Keep on winding until the hole in the middle of the ring is filled with yarn (you may need to cut additional strands to do this). When it gets difficult to pull the yarn through with your fingers you can use the crochet hook.

4. Cut the yarn all the way around the two rings and tie a piece of strong, thick thread between the two cardboard rings with a tight knot. Remove the cardboard rings to reveal a hedgehog-like pom-pom (fig. 2).

5. To make the hedgehog's head cut a pie shape from the felt. Fold it in half and sew the two straight sides together.

6. Fill the shape with your stuffing and sew a felt circle over the base of the cone so that the stuffing doesn't come out (fig. 3).

7. Glue the head on to the pom-pom body and secure with a few stitches.

8. Make the nose by sewing a few stitches over the tip of the cone using thick black thread. Sew on two buttons for eyes or simply make two black blobs with thread.

9. Glue a long doweling rod in between the hedgehog's head and body. Place a piece of cloth over a chair, hold the hedgehog-puppet by the rod and move him along. He can make very swift little steps or sniff along slowly, disappear and come out again, find some fruit… the possibilities are endless.

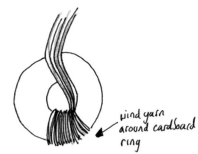

wind yarn around cardboard ring

figure 1

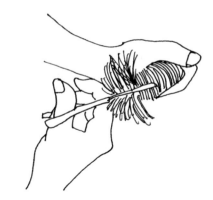

figure 2

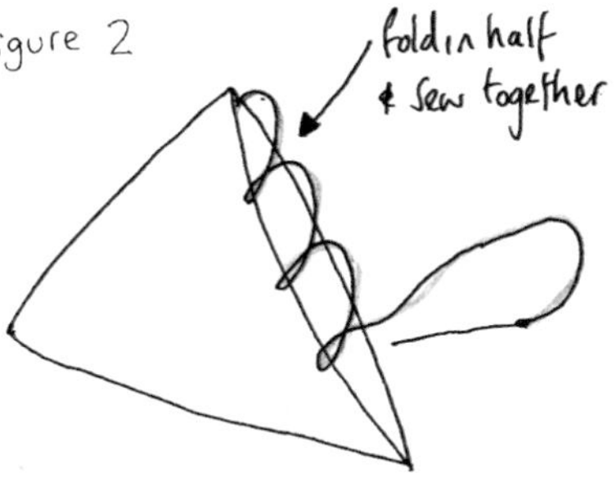

fold in half & sew together

figure 3

Sooz Fry

HANGING IN THE BALANCE

This mesmerising mobile has a very simple structure that emphasises balance and movement. Stars and planets hang in the balance with a mix of wet felted wool balls and sewn felt stars, with a few beads thrown in for fun. Hang the finished item above a child or baby's bed and they will be bound to have cosmic dreams.

Materials

+ Wire coat hanger or other wire
+ Pliers with wire cutters
+ Wool fleece in a range of colours as well as undyed
+ Bowls with hot soapy and cold water
+ Small squares of felt
+ Needles and cotton, including one very long or 'doll making' needle
+ Beads or other embellishments
+ Fishing line or strong thread
+ Hot glue gun (optional)

Instructions

1. Snip the three straight sides from the coat hanger and bend the ends to loops. Make sure the loops face the same way and the finished bent wire sits flat (fig. 1).

2. Using fishing line attach the shorter pieces (the lower tier) and the longer piece (the upper tier). Use the loops on the upper tier and tie the line roughly in the centre of the lower pieces. Don't worry about being too precise—you will be adjusting the exact location of the line on the lower tiers once the objects are attached.

3. To make the felt balls, start by choosing your colour palette from dyed wool rovings. This mobile makes use of warm yellows, oranges and reds, but cool colours also look great.

4. Prepare two bowls of water for the felting. Fill one with hot soapy water, the other with clean cool water. Smaller balls can be made in a single step. Take a handful of wool fleece and roll it up tight into a ball. Dip it into the hot water until it is fully wet and then gently roll it between your palms. As you roll, the wool will gradually shrink and harden to felt. As it firms you can apply an increasing amount of pressure. Occasionally dip it again into the soapy water to keep it wet, and if it becomes too soapy rinse it with a dip in the cool water. When the ball is firmly felted rinse in the cool water, roll out excess moisture on a paper towel and leave to dry.

5. For bigger balls start with a core of undyed wool fleece. You can use coloured wool, but as you won't see this inner layer it is more economical to use undyed wool. Make a small ball as before and add a 'skin' by covering your ball with a mat of wool that is roughly even in thickness. Dip the covered ball in the hot water and roll between your palms as before. As you start the skin will be much looser than the underlying ball—be gentle and work the skin evenly as it shrinks.

6. When the balls are dry, thread each one on to a length of fishing line using a long strong needle such as a doll making needle. You can add beads or other decorations to the line if you wish (fig. 2).

7. To make your other objects, choose a simple shape, like a star, and cut this from felt (you can either buy felt or make it yourself—see page 24). For each object you will need two matching shapes to sew together.

8. Embellish your shapes before you sew them together. Try contrasting felt shapes, beads and flower shaped sequins on the stars. Stitch the two shapes together using a blanket stitch (see page 26), and stuff with fleece or fibrefill.

9. Once the objects are complete, thread on lengths of fishing line, again adding beads or other decorative items if you wish.

10. Assemble the mobile by adding objects to each of the loops on the lower tiers, and one centrally to each of the three wire structures. This mobile is symetrical, with balls hanging off each loop and stars hanging from the centres, but you can just as easily create beautiful asymmetrical mobiles by adding more, or heavier objects, at one end of the supporting wires.

11. Once all the objects are attached, hang the mobile from a doorframe or other free standing position and adjust for balance. Do this by sliding the fishing lines in the centres of the wires to the side until the objects on that wire hang in balance. When all the lines are correctly placed and in balance, place a small dot of glue from the hot glue gun over the lines to secure their position (all-purpose glue will do, but you'll need to close the window so it doesn't move as it dries).

figure 1

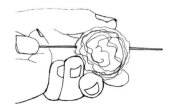

figure 2

figure 3

About Sooz

Sooz is a craftsperson working in Melbourne, Australia, who makes practical, durable pieces, including clothing, jewellery and quilts that bring a little handmade beauty to everyday things. With the birth of her first child, Sooz became interested in toys and other objects for children that are centred on natural materials, particularly felts, and offer opportunities for imaginative and interactive play. She sells her creations through her online shop *www.sooz.com* and blogs about her craft ventures at *www.soozs.blogspot.com*

Joanna Miller
CURTAIN SPIDERS

These nasty little bugs are easy to make, and are a great hit with the kids. Make them on Halloween, or any other grey afternoon when you need a distraction activity. The springy ones, especially, can provide hours of entertainment.

Materials
+ 8 plastic curtain hooks
+ Blue tac
+ Small plastic curtain ring
    (around 2.5 cm in diameter)
    or 1 pipe cleaner
+ Black shearing elastic
+ Black acrylic paint
+ Thin elastic (optional)
+ Large curtain ring (optional)

Instructions

1. Take the small curtain ring and slot the curtain hooks on one by one, until you have put on all eight hooks. If you don't have a curtain ring, make your own by cutting a length of pipe cleaner 9 cm long. Make a circle approximately 2.5 cm wide, and twist the ends around each other. Attach the curtain hooks as above.

2. Turn upside down and press a blob of blue tac into the centre, using enough blue tac that it touches all the legs and fills the ring.

3. Turn it back the right way up and put another blob of blue tac on top. Mould this with your fingers until you have a shape you are happy with for the body of your spider. If you want a line down the centre of the spider's body, create an indent in the blue tac by pressing the edge of a plastic ruler into it.

4. Paint the spider on one side. Leave this to dry and then turn the spider over to paint the other side. Be sure to take your time and paint inside all the curves on the curtain hooks. Acrylic paint works best for this, but if you want to use powder paint with young children, mix some washing up liquid into it, so that it adheres better to the plastic (1½ tsp of washing up liquid per ½ cup of powder).

Tips

+ Turn your spider into an arm band or bracelet by knotting elastic onto two legs opposite each other.

+ Turn your spider into a springy spider by knotting a piece of thin elastic to a leg on one end, and to a large curtain ring on the other. Paint the ring black.

About Joanna

Joanna is an artist working across many different disciplines. Her interest in new materials and processes led her to get involved in craft. She has worked in the craft industry testing new materials before they were put on the market. In recent years, she has worked within the community, teaching and running creative workshops with adults and children, helping them develop their creativity alongside her own.

Mark Butcher
JACKITO-LANTERNS

These itty bitty little babies are so much easier to carve than those great big pumpkins, and when you put the tea light inside, they fill the room with a luscious citrus fragrance.

Materials
+ 1 orange
+ 1 tea light
+ Small sharp knife
+ Teaspoon

Instructions

1. Take one orange and cut off the very top in a zigzag pattern. Remove the top and use the spoon to dig out the contents (save this to eat later).

2. Draw a face on the orange with a pen. Then use the sharp knife to cut out the mouth and the eyes. Keep it simple as you have only a little space to work with.

3. Take the top of the orange that you cut off in step 1, and cut a small hole in the middle. This will serve as the chimney, so your orange doesn't smoulder and go black.

4. Place the tea light in the base of the orange and fit the top back on (try and match up the zigzags).

Tips

+ Make a whole crew of jackito-lanterns—they look great on a fireplace or lining the way along a path to your front door on Halloween. Then make a jug of fresh orange juice from the leftovers.

+ Clementines work just as well, but as they're smaller, you'll need a steady hand.

About Mark

See page 76 for bio.

STEINER DOLLS

Steiner dolls have their origins in nineteenth century Germany. They are very simple, faceless dolls, made with scraps of cotton and felt and stuffed with sheep's wool. They were appropriated by Rudolf Steiner who admired their simplicity and used them as an educational tool. There's something deeply comforting about a Steiner doll, and they're always a big hit with the kids.

Materials

+ Good quality wool felt
+ 1 old t-shirt
  (preferably flesh toned)
+ Stuffing
+ A chopstick (or another thin
  implement for stuffing)
+ Pins and needles
+ Regular sewing thread
+ Optional decorative elements such
  as tiny buttons, embroidery floss,
  little bells, and wool for hair

Instructions

1. Cut a pattern for the body: You can use the pattern overleaf as a guide (fig. 1). This is for small standing dolls with a flat base (10 cm tall), but feel free to vary it.

2. Cut out two body pieces from your felt for each doll. Thick felt can sometimes be quite difficult to cut, so you might want to cut one first and then cut the second using the first as a guide (felt tends to stick together, so this should be fairly easy). There's no need to leave a seam allowance as they will be blanket stitched on the outside. Don't worry if it's not precise—they're supposed to be a little rough and ready.

3. Make a head sleeve from the t-shirt material. You want it to be about 5 cm long for this size doll, and when sewn, about 2.5 cm wide (about 1 cm wider than the body neck hole). If you have a machine handy that's fine, if not a hand sewn back stitch seam is fine too (you won't see this seam later).

4. Embellish your bodies if you want. Remember these guys are meant to be simple—a few stitches to imply buttons (or if toddler safety isn't an issue some actual tiny buttons), a simple flower or a star is enough.

5. Blanket stitch around the body leaving the neck open (see page 26).

6. Stuff the body, starting with the limbs. Stuff as much as you possibly can... and then stuff some more. The dolls need to be plump and firm and they will compact a bit. Leave just enough of a hollow in the neck to get the head in.

7. Close off the top of the head sleeve with a running stitch 1 mm away from the top edge of your sleeve. Gather in tight and tie off securely.

8. Turn the head inside out and then stuff. Use another running stitch to hold the stuffing in place, making sure the head is really firm and well stuffed. Soft is not good.

9. Add another running stitch above the first (fig. 2)—this will form a neck for the head and make the head stuffing even firmer, preventing the head-to-neck join from being weak and floppy.

10. Push the head into the neck hole and sew in place. If both the head and body are well stuffed, this will require some force. Use the stuffing stick to really push it in amongst the body stuffing. The deeper into the body you can get the head the better the neck join will be. Stitch the head and body together. You can use any stitch you like to do this, so long as it is strong and relatively even. Your basic doll is now complete!

11. Cut a hat. Measure the circumference of the head from front forehead to the nape of the neck, with enough height to cover the head. You'll end up with a shape something like the one in fig. 3. There is no end to the styles of hats you can make though, so be creative!

12. Sew up and attach the hat using a blanket stitch from the bottom edge to the top point of the hat. Then back stitch down the seam, pulling in to gather as you go. Back stitch around the hat rim, securing it to the head.

Hair

You may want to add hair to your doll. Like hats, hair has endless variations. Carded or uncarded fleece, silk fibre and knitting yarns all make excellent hair and can be left as loose flowing locks, trimmed short or tied in bunches or plaits.

13. Attach the wool to the head from crown to nape with secure stitches. Plait the hair and tie off using a needle to pull thread through the fibres to ensure ties don't slip off.

14. Attach the hat, in this case a kerchief style using the same basic method as the hat above but instead of a curve above the head, taper sides to a point.

15. Get carried away. Steiner dolls are traditionally faceless, though you can add a little stitch on either side of the face to imply eyes. Add a bell on top of the hat, or sew a little sleeping bag from felt (kids love this).

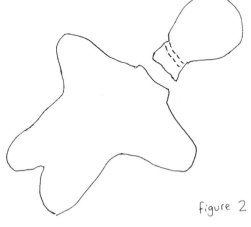

figure 2

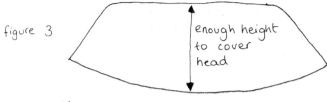

figure 3

enough height
to cover
head

Hat template suggestion

1cm

□ 1cm

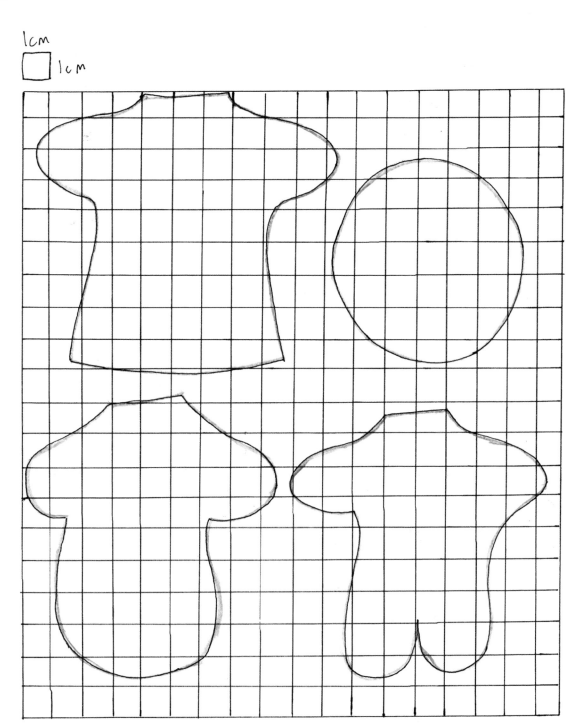

figure 1

About Sooz

See page 118 for bio.

Dr Sara Robb

BEESWAX CANDLES

Rolled beeswax candles are fun to make and have a lovely subtle honey smell. They have that rustic *je ne sais quoi*, and make great gifts. You don't need any special equipment and they can be made without any fragrance or heat, so it's an ideal activity for younger children.

Materials

+ Beeswax sheets—these can be bought at most craft shops, or online
+ Candle wicks—ideally pre-waxed
+ Cutting board
+ Pizza cutter (optional)
+ Ruler
+ Scissors

Instructions

1. Select one sheet of beeswax and a wick. The length of the wick should be slightly longer than the beeswax sheet. If the wick is quite short, trim the beeswax with scissors or the pizza cutter.

2. Place the wick at the end of the beeswax sheet so it is square with the bottom and there is 1 cm of wick extending from the other end. The side with the flush wick is the bottom of the candle. The side with the extended wick is the top.

3. Begin to roll the beeswax sheet around the wick. Try to roll the candle so the spiral is tight, keeping both ends even. This is a bit tricky. If the candle starts to go a bit crooked, simply unroll, back up and try again.

4. Continue to roll until you reach the end of the sheet of beeswax.

5. To finish the candle, use gentle pressure to push the edge of the beeswax sheet into the candle to create a seam.

6. If you want to embellish your candle, select a contrasting colour of beeswax and cut out a flower shape—six hexagons around a centre hexagon create a flower pattern.

7. Tear tiny pieces of wax, the same colour as the candle (or a different colour) and roll them into small balls. Place the balls in the centre of each flower and press the flowers gently into the candle to make them stick.

About Dr Sara

See page 87 for bio

Hannah Ayre

ABBEY BABY BIB

Whether you like it or not, you will get to an age (if you haven't got there already) when your friends will start having babies at a rate of knots! This bib makes a great personalised gift for new parents. This one was made entirely from scraps of fabric—but try laminated fabric or thick plastic for a mess-proof version.

Materials

+ Fabric and matching thread
+ 6 cm of Velcro
+ Sewing machine (or could be done by hand if you have the patience)
+ Pair of compasses or 9 cm round implement, such as a mug

Instructions

1. To create the pattern, draw an oval shape approximately. 30 cm high by 24 cm wide on a piece of paper. Fold it in half vertically with the pencil lines showing on the outside. Cut it out, while it's still folded. This ensures the design will be symmetrical.

2. Open the pattern out flat. 2 cm down from the top of the pattern draw a circle of about 9 cm in diameter, using a compass or a large mug as a guide. The fold mark should appear in the centre of this circle. This will create the hole for the baby's head.

3. Cut the circle out, cutting through the 2 cm top of the pattern. The two ends created will make the neck straps. They can be rounded off with scissors for a better shape.

4. Place the pattern onto your fabric, draw round it and cut out.

5. For the pocket, use your existing pattern, and from the bottom measure 10 cm along the centre fold. At this point draw a straight line at a right angle to the centre fold all the way across the pattern, then cut along this line. You should now have a half moon shape. Place this onto your fabric, draw round and cut out.

6. For the baby's name cut out the letters from a different fabric. Pin them onto the front of the pocket section a little way in from the edges. The letters can then be stitched on either with a tight zigzag stitch on the machine, or by hand (see page 25 for appliqué techniques).

7. Next create the edging for the bib using thin strips of fabric.

The first strip needs to be the length of the straight edge of the pocket, so measure and cut out a piece approximately 5 cm wide (the length should work out at about 24 cm). Using an iron, create three creases down the length of this. To do this, fold the fabric in half lengthways with the pattern showing on the outside and iron. Unfold the fabric and fold the two outside edges in to meet the central crease. Iron again. Keeping the folds in place, fold in half again down the centre of the fabric and iron all the layers flat. You should now have a piece of edging about 12 mm wide by 24 cm in length.

8. Sandwich the top flat edge of the bib pocket between this edging, pin and stitch along the edge through all layers of the fabric.

9. Using the same technique in step 7, create edging to go around the entire bib. This will need to be approximately 5 × 126 cm. This can be all in one length or several smaller scraps of fabric put together.

10. Place the pocket onto the front of the bib and pin down. Work around the bib pinning on the edging. Be sure to sandwich both the main fabric and the pocket into the edging. It is a little tricky to fit the edging around the curves, using an iron will help, and make small tucks if needed. Stitch in place.

11. Stitch Velcro onto the tabs at the top of the bib.

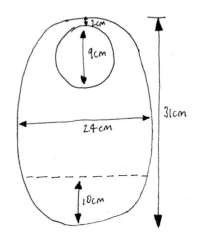

About Hannah

See page 78 for bio.

Natalie Abbott
PIXIE BONNET

This delightful pointed pixie bonnet is perfect for impish youngsters. It makes use of a mix of knitting and felting, allowing you to indulge in some no-brainer knitting, as the shaping is worked by cutting and sewing the material post-felt. Designed for age 12–30 months.

Materials

+ 100% wool 3–4 ply yarn
+ Knitting needles
+ Needle and thread
+ Button

Instructions

1. Always knit a test square to make sure your yarn will felt well before starting the project. Check the gauge, written on the front of your yarn and knit a 10 × 10 cm square (see page 19).

2. Shrinkage on different yarns will vary, so felt your test square and measure it again to give you the accurate end size in relation to the original 10 cm square. To hand felt your knitting, you will need a bowl of very hot water about 4 cm deep. (as the water in the bowl cools, dispose of it and replace with fresh very hot water). Wear rubber gloves so you don't burn yourself. Add soap powder, and sprinkle this on your knitting. Rub the knitting together, agitating the fibres. You could also try rubbing the yarn with bubble wrap. You will start to notice the texture of the knitting change and eventually the visible knitting structure will start to disappear. The swatch should now be anything from 20–50% smaller than the original.

3. Your templates laid out have a combined measurement of 25 × 67 cm. Divide these numbers by the end size of the felted swatch and then multiply your original cast on quantities by the results:

   Number of stitches cast on for 10 × 10 cm swatch multiplied by 25, divided by the felted size of the swatch = number of stitches to cast on.

   Number of rows knitted for 10 × 10 cm swatch multiplied by 67, divided by the felted size of the swatch = number of rows to knit.

   So if your gauge for a 10 × 10 cm swatch was 26 stitches and 34 rows, and your felted swatch measured 5 × 5 cm, you would cast on 130 stitches and knit 456 rows.

4. Knit in stockinette stitch as required and felt your final piece. It should now be 25 × 67 cm.

5. Steam your felted fabric by placing a damp cloth over it as you iron.

6. Redraw the patterns on the right to the specified dimensions (they should be able to squeeze onto A4 sheets—although you might have to stick two sheets together for the top section), pin onto your fabric and cut out, (remember you will need two side pieces).

7. Sew the longest edge of both side sections to either side of the long edge of the top section. Leave a 5 mm seam allowance (seam allowances do not need to be doubled over as your felt will not fray). This is easiest on a sewing machine, but if you do not have access to one, double your thread and use small, neat stitches.

8. Fold the top section in the middle lengthways. Your bonnet should now be symmetrical and inside out. Sew the slanted edge of the side sections and top together leaving a 5 mm seam allowance. This has now created the back seam and bonnet peak. Sew around the front edge and bottom of the bonnet, leaving a seam allowance.

9. Turn your bonnet the right way around and place your fastening strip on the bottom right hand side of the bonnet. Sew into place.

10. Sew a button of your choice on the opposite side of the bonnet and cut a slit in the fastening strap the appropriate size for the button (felt doesn't fray, so no complicated buttonhole sewing!).

11. You now have your finished pixie bonnet and are free to decorate it as you wish. Sew on circles or flower shapes with oddments of yarn using a blanket stitch, use buttons or appliqué scrap material.

Tip

+ Can't be bothered with the knitting? Just skip steps 1–5 and felt an old jumper instead (see page 24).

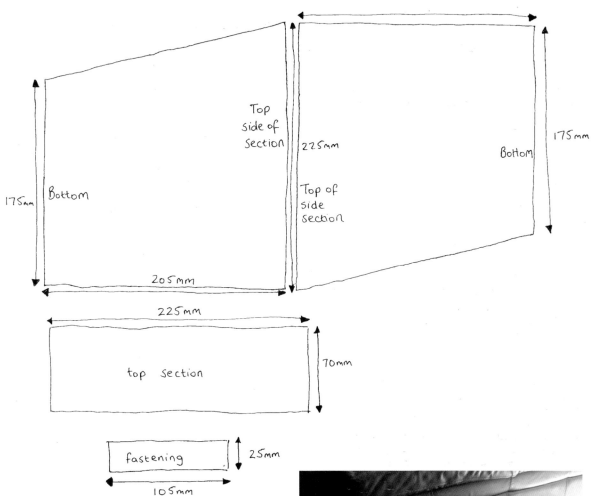

Top
side of
Section

225mm

175mm

Bottom

Top of
side
Section

175mm

Bottom

175mm

Bottom

205mm

225mm

top section

70mm

fastening

25mm

105mm

About Natalie

Natalie finished her textiles degree in 2002. She had her first child in 2003, and promptly decided that children's wear was the direction in which she wanted to progress. Her website, *www.toxicpixie.co.uk* offers a fun alternative (especially for newborns) to traditional baby kitsch. She has recently delved into the world of adult accessories—she couldn't let children have all the fun! She also freelances and helps run textile based workshops for children.

Victoria Woodcock
FROCK ROCKING IN SMOCKING

Smocking makes the simplest dress pattern fit to the body without calling for darts, buttons and zips. It is a fun technique to try out on a sewing machine and impresses people because it doesn't look 'handmade'. It works equally well for a child or an adult. Who'd have thought it—smocking is good for you!

Materials

+ Cotton fabric (see below to calculate how much)
+ Matching coloured thread
+ Spool of shearing elastic (a similar colour to the fabric)
+ Tailors' chalk
+ Sewing machine

Instructions

1. Measurements: measure the person the dress is intended for. You need three measurements, around the chest, from underneath your armpit to where you want the hem to fall, and the length of the area you want to smock. The smocking will pull the fabric in tight across the body and where it ends it will billow out, so for a child's dress you probably want the smocking down to the waist. To create an empire line dress, smock to the ribs.

   So for 3-year-old Amelia:
   Chest: 53 cm, Top to hem: 46 cm, Smocking: 15 cm

   For an adult, UK size 12:
   Chest: 91 cm, Top to hem: 76 cm,
   Smocking: 28 cm (to waist) 15 cm (empire line)

2. Now work out the width of your pattern:
   Chest measurement ÷ 4 = x
   Chest + x = y
   y ÷ 2 = z

   For Amelia, z = 33 cm

3. You are going to make this dress in two parts and it is going to flair out at the hem into an A-line shape. With your measurements draw out a pattern—commercial patterns work in halves but initially when making your own it's easier to make the whole shape. On a large piece of paper, draw a rectangle with z as the width and the top to hem measurement as the length. Draw a line across at the point you want the smocking to reach. See fig. 1 overleaf for pattern.

4. Make the A-line by extending the bottom edge of the rectangle on either side. The greater the length of these extensions the more 'body' the skirt will have. Adding a third of the z measurement either side will give a nice shape. For Amelia's frock, 11.5 cm were added on either side to make a hem length of 56 cm. Use a ruler to draw diagonal lines from where the smocking lines reach the edge of the rectangle (A) to the points you have just made (B). Measure the distance from the waist to the hem (A–C, here 31 cm) and measure this distance from point A along the diagonal. Mark this point (D). Join points D and C with a gentle curve. Repeat on the other side and cut out your pattern (see overleaf for a basic pattern).

5. Pin the pattern to the fabric, so that the top edge faces towards one cut edge and runs along the weave of the fabric. Draw around it in chalk and repeat (technically what you should do is fold the fabric, draw half the pattern and cut. Do whatever works for you.) Cut out the two pieces, allowing 2.5 cm selvedge all around for seams and hemming.

6. Draw horizontal lines in chalk at 1 cm intervals on the right side of the body sections. Pin the two pieces right sides together, taking care to line up the corners. Sew along the side seams.

7. Make a V-shaped cut where the skirt begins to stick out and press the seams flat. To hem the top, fold the fabric to just before the chalk line, iron and then fold again on the chalk line. Iron again and sew into place. Because the skirt has a slight curve at the hem, the smaller the amount of fabric folded over the better—here it is easier to fold on the chalk line first, cut any excess fabric, tuck under the rough edges, press and pin into place. If you find there is excess material in the fold around the curve, cut a few slender V-shapes from the selvedge, so that they fall neatly on top of one another rather than bunching up.

8. To smock, set the stitch length on your machine to 4 (or the longest length). Wind the shearing elastic onto the bobbin and use the same cotton as before as the top thread. Now just sew around the chalk lines and watch it pucker up. The first circle may be on the hem and with the thickness of fabric will not scrunch up very much. If this happens, sew an extra round just a few millimetres away from the edge of the fabric.

9. Make straps that fasten in bows using either ribbon or making them from the fabric. To do so, cut 4 strips 4 × 50 cm, place one on the ironing board right side down. Fold the two edges over so that they meet in the middle and iron. Fold in half again and press. Sew a line along the strip, tucking in the rough edges at the ends.

10. To position the straps, get the model to try on the dress and mark where they should go. Attach the straps by sewing over them a couple of times along the first and second lines of smocking.

+ You can make an even easier dress by skipping the A-line shape and by working with just the initial rectangle shape. This isn't really any good for little children as they won't be able to run around in it. Just make sure that your hips or belly aren't bigger than your 'y' measurement. Make it strapless or add wide straps. Make it shorter for a top or add a waist tie to an empire line.

Buying the right amount of fabric

+ For an adult sized dress, the hem can only be as wide as the fabric you use. To make a size 12 A-line dress, the hem width would be approximately 95 cm (calculate it by adding a third of the z measurement to either side) so you would need a fabric at least 1 m in width and twice the length of the top to hem distance—about 2 m.

+ For a little dress you may be able to fit the pattern pieces side by side along one width and you will only need to buy the length from top to hem with selvedge. In order to calculate the minimum width of the fabric for you to do this, just double the hem length and add 10 cm for selvedge. For Amelia, the fabric needs to be at least 122 cm wide. Then you just need to buy the length of the top to hem including selvedges, plus a little extra for the straps—in this case 60 cm. When starting out, always overestimate the amount of fabric you'll need (in this case, you should probably buy 1 m just to be sure— if there's any fabric left over you can always make a matching bag).

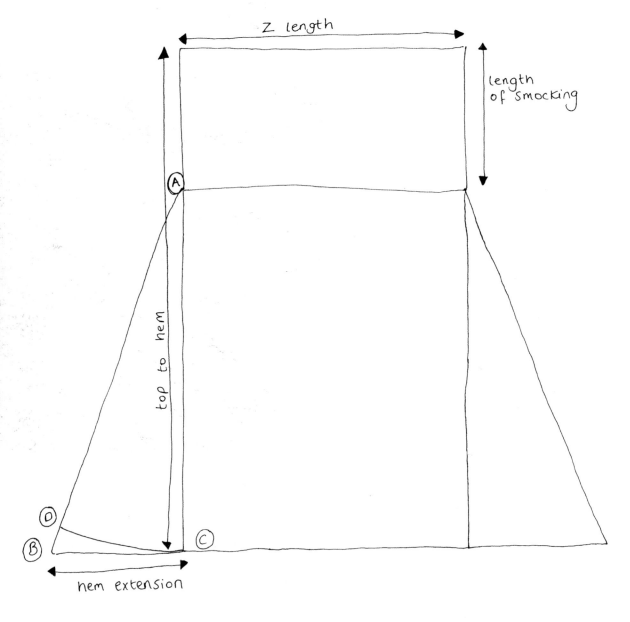

Richard Mansfield
UMBRELLA SHADOW SHOW

Puppetry is currently experiencing a bit of a revival; public awareness is growing of puppetry as an art form and it is increasingly becoming available to adults as well as children. Making a shadow puppet theatre from an umbrella is quick, cheap, portable and heaps of fun!

Materials

+ 1 umbrella in a pale shade — ideally white
+ 1 large, powerful torch
+ Gaffer tape
+ Black card
+ Split pins
+ Thin dowelling rod or thin cane
+ Velcro
+ Scalpel or craft knife

Instructions

1. Open the umbrella, and gaffer tape the torch to the end of the handle so that you can hold the brolly and torch together. When switched on the torch light should fill the umbrella. This is your theatre!

2. Design your characters on paper and trace them onto the black card. Remember, if you want to make eyes, a mouth or any other detail, then you will need to cut these out so the light can shine through. You can colour your cut-out sections with cellophane if you like. Think about what characters you need to tell a story. This puppet show involved a spaceman, an alien, a shooting star and a spaceship.

3. If you want to create moving parts, cut out the piece you want to move (i.e. an arm or leg) separately and attach it to the main body of the puppet with a split pin.

4. By attaching the shadow puppet to a rod, you can operate it easily, whilst holding the umbrella in place. Take a long dowelling rod and a small square of Velcro. Stick the harder hook side of the Velcro to the end of the rod, and the soft loop side to the puppet. Do this with a couple of rods, so that you can operate a number of puppets simultaneously. If you don't have Velcro, gaffer tape will do.

5. Turn out the lights, turn on the torch, and let the show begin! A complicated story may require a puppet-master's assistant to help operate the puppets.

About Richard

Richard has always been interested in the human form, in particular puppets. He studied model design, but most of his skills as a maker are self-taught. He uses a lot of papier mâché pulp to make his figures because it is cheap, easy to use and relatively non-toxic. He is a budding filmmaker and enjoys creating an intimate, alternate world the puppets can share with their audience. *www.bonbichiepuppets.co.uk*

Kate MacKay

ECO WARRIOR KITE

The design of traditional Asian kites is inspired by the natural structures of leaves and birds, and they are beautiful objects as well as powerful structures. They were originally intended for use in battles, so Kate designed this kite with use in protest marches in mind. Using recycled urban materials this kite will fly in the face of adversity as well as fly through the air.

Materials

+ 1 bamboo blind—these can be found in lots of charity shops or picked up cheaply in furniture warehouses
+ Strong plastic bags or bubble wrap (the air in the bubble wrap makes the kite fly really well)
+ Tape: insulating tape from hardware stores is really good, although sticky tape can also be used effectively
+ Raffia, or light durable string
+ Fabric, plastic or ribbon scraps

Instructions

1. Fold a large piece of paper (A2) in half, and cut out a symmetrical template (fig.1).

2. Lay the template across the crease of the plastic bag or on folded over bubble wrap.

2. Draw around it, cut it out, and then open out the symmetrical bird shape (fig. 2).

3. Cut some bamboo rods off the blind, and lay one down the centre crease of the kite from beak to tail. Tape along its length.

4. Cut a bamboo rod 2.5 cm longer than the wingspan. Tape it down at each wing tip so that there is a slight curve across the wingspan and the plastic is taught. Again, tape along its length (to protect the bamboo from snapping).

5. Cut two bamboo rods to go from the cross of the centre rod and the wing span rod, to halfway along the wing, creating a diagonal support across the wings. Tape this as before (fig. 4).

6. Cut 2 small pieces of bamboo and tape them diagonally on either side of the tail.

7. Make two holes at either side of the centre rod at the point where the wing and centre rods cross, and another two holes at the base of the centre rod, before the tail, either side of the centre rod.

8. Cut a piece of string about .5 m long. Thread one end in and out of the top holes and tie the end to the same piece of string close to the back of the kite. Thread the other end of the string in and out of the bottom holes and tie in the same way. This creates the harness.

9. Cut a long piece of string—the length of this string will determine how high your kite will fly, so make sure it's good and long. Attach it to the middle of the harness with a loose loop so that it can be moved up and down to adjust the flying.

10. Attach long ribbons, plastic, or scraps with tape for the tail. The tail helps the kite balance and fly, it's not just for decoration!

11. Decorate the kite as you wish—slogans or painted wings go down a treat—and fly it anywhere and everywhere.

figure 1

figure 2

figure 3

figure 4

About Kate

The transformation of materials from waste back into product is a process that has always fascinated Kate, and she set up an artists' collective and scrap store called Alchemy Arts to encourage creative recycling. Since their establishment, Alchemy Arts have been commissioned to create public art all around Edinburgh, as well as running workshops in festivals throughout Europe. Kate believes that craft "can profoundly enhance the way we view ourselves and the world around us... through the transformation of perceptions and materials, we have the potential to transform our sense of self, of others and of our environment."